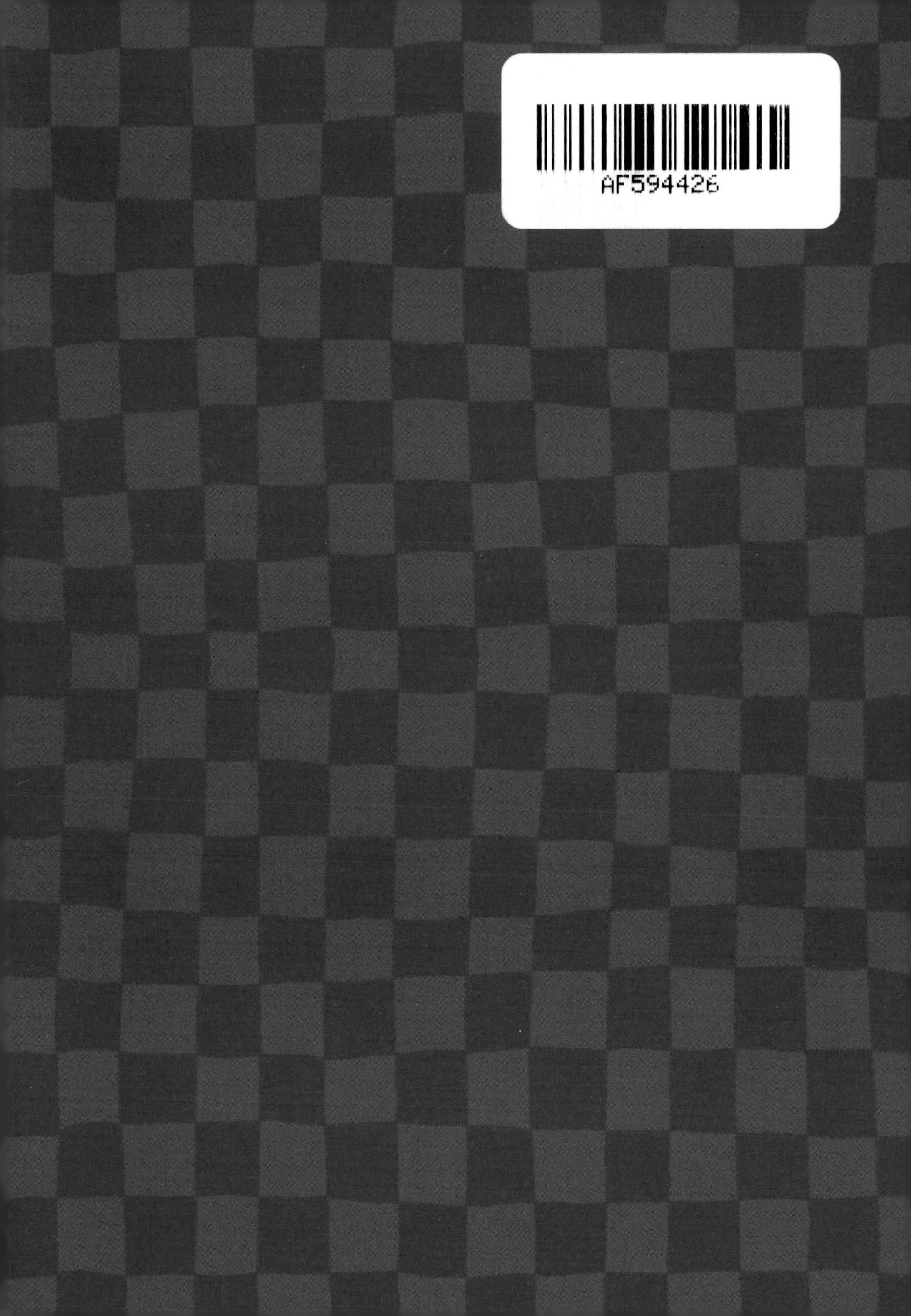
AF594426

THIS IS TERRIBLE THIS IS WONDERFUL

DISPATCHES FROM THE POSTPARTUM UNIVERSE

WORDS & ART BY RANI BAN

QUIRK BOOKS
PHILADELPHIA

FULL LIBRARY OF CONGRESS CATALOGING-IN-PUBLICATION DATA AVAILABLE UPON REQUEST.

ISBN: 978-1-68369-498-4

PRINTED IN CHINA

ART DIRECTION BY ANDIE REID
PRODUCTION MANAGEMENT BY MANDY SAMPSON

QUIRK BOOKS
215 CHURCH STREET
PHILADELPHIA, PA 19106
QUIRKBOOKS.COM

QUIRK BOOKS' AUTHORIZED REPRESENTATIVE IN THE EU FOR PRODUCT SAFETY AND COMPLIANCE IS EASY ACCESS SYSTEM EUROPE, MUSTAMÄE TEE 50, 10621 TALLINN, ESTONIA, GPSR.REQUESTS@EASPROJECT.COM.

10 9 8 7 6 5 4 3 2 1

CONTENTS:

DEAR PERSON WHO NOW HAS A BABY,

I MADE THIS BOOK FOR YOU.

THIS BOOK WILL NOT TELL YOU HOW TO THRIVE IN THE FIRST YEAR OF HAVING A BABY BECAUSE I DON'T KNOW HOW TO DO THAT. THIS BOOK <u>WILL</u> TELL YOU THAT YOU'RE NOT ALONE IF YOU AREN'T THRIVING.

AS I WROTE THE FOLLOWING ESSAYS &

OFF-KILTER POEMS, THEY TOOK ME PLACES FAR AND WIDE, IN THIS WORLD AND BEYOND.

POSTPARTUM LOOKS SO COZY AND DOMESTIC FROM THE OUTSIDE, BUT ON THE INSIDE I WAS IN FAR-OFF PLACES. IT FELT LIKE BEING UNTETHERED IN OUTER SPACE, FELT LIKE TENDING TO A GARDEN WITH SNAKES UNDERFOOT, FELT LIKE ANCIENT ROMAN MYTHOLOGY, AND FELT LIKE NAVIGATING THE WILD SEA WITHOUT A COMPASS.

I FELT OVERWHELMING COMPASSION FOR MY POSTPARTUM SELF AS I TRAVELED FAR AND WIDE TO ARTICULATE HER EXPERIENCE. I'VE CRIED FOR HER, MADE SPACE FOR HER, CELEBRATED HER, AND WISHED I COULD GO BACK AND SAY:

"WHAT YOU ARE DOING IS REALLY HARD!"

I GUESS WHAT I MEAN IS,

I WISH I COULD GO BACK IN TIME AND HAND HER THIS BOOK.

I LEARNED SO MUCH THAT FIRST YEAR EVEN THOUGH IT DIDN'T FEEL LIKE IT.

IT WAS A COMPLETELY IMMERSIVE, INTIMATE, AND ISOLATING EXPERIENCE THAT DIDN'T MAKE ME FEEL A 19TH-CENTURY OIL PAINTING OF MOTHER & CHILD. IN FACT, IT MADE ME FEEL LIKE A SWOLLEN & DAMP GOBLIN AT THE FOOT OF A MOUNTAIN THAT I DIDN'T HAVE THE STRENGTH TO CLIMB.

HERE ARE SOME ESSAYS AND POEMS ABOUT MY POST-PARTUM EXPERIENCE— DISPATCHES FROM MY BEDROOM AND FAR BEYOND.

I HOPE THIS BOOK MAKES SPACE FOR THE SPECIFICITY AND GRAVITY OF WHAT YOU'RE GOING THROUGH.

BECAUSE THIS—

THIS IS TERRIBLE
THIS IS WONDERFUL

AND ONE DOESN'T
CANCEL OUT THE OTHER.

WITH OVERWHELMING COMPASSION,
RANI

PART 1:
THE
COSMOS

FOR A WHILE I FELT LIKE I WAS FLOATING ABOVE EARTH INSTEAD OF LIVING ON IT. TIME BECAME AN AMORPHOUS CONCEPT INSTEAD OF A RELIABLE PATTERN. NO RISING WITH THE SUN OR RESTING WHEN IT SET.

WE WERE ATTACHED TO EACH OTHER AND FLOATED SO FAR INTO THE COSMOS I DIDN'T KNOW IF WE'D BE ABLE TO FIND OUR WAY BACK.

IF YOU'RE FLOATING TOO,

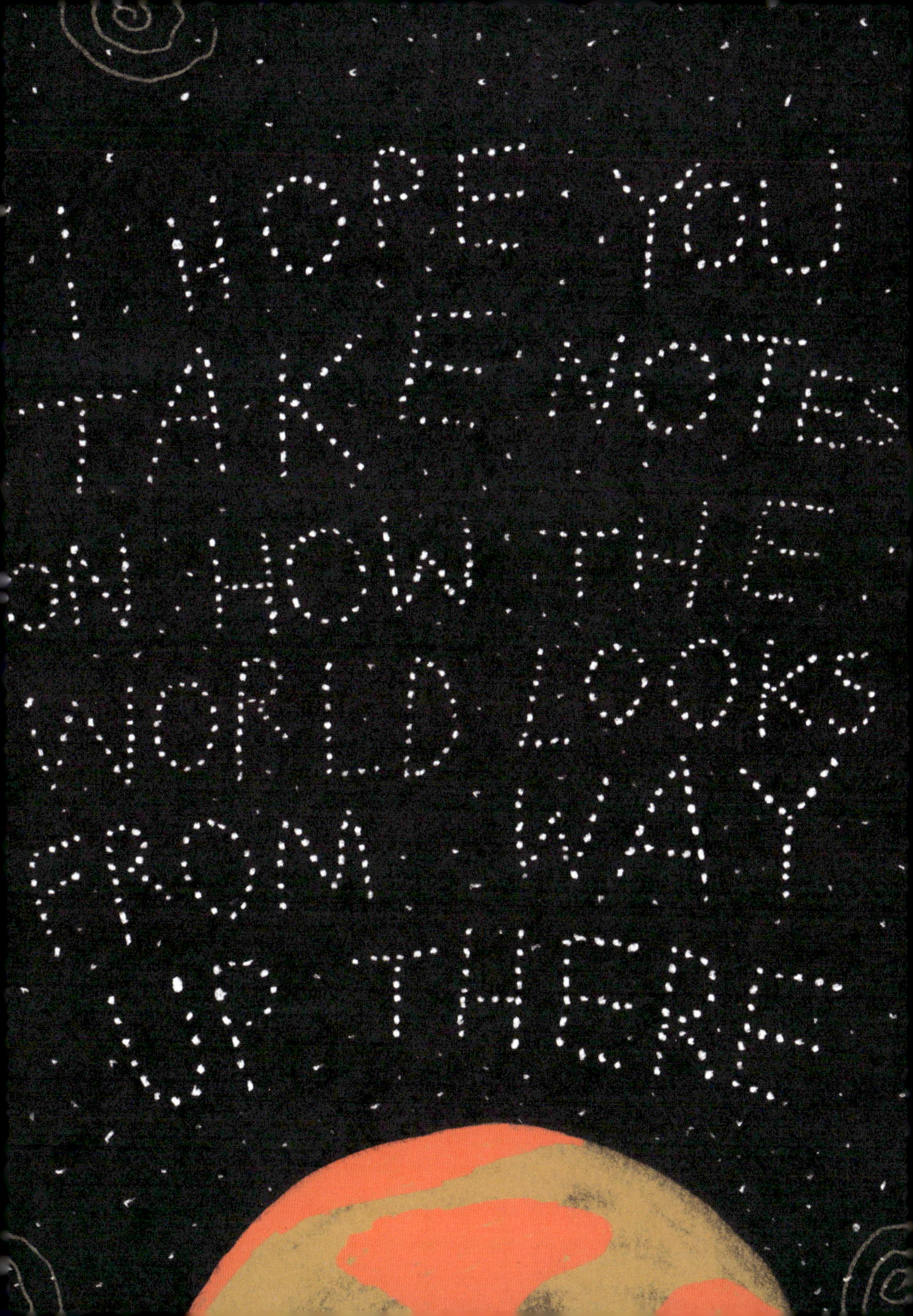
I HOPE YOU
TAKE NOTES
ON HOW THE
WORLD LOOKS
FROM WAY
UP THERE

CRICKET

IT'S 3 A.M. AND MY
EYES ARE A LITTLE
BLURRY FROM
CRYING.

"IT'S ALL TOO MUCH"
"IT FEELS
IMPOSSIBLE"

"I THINK THERE'S SOMETHING WRONG WITH ME"

I TELL MY BOYFRIEND AND HE LISTENS. I HADN'T SLEPT MUCH RECENTLY AND THAT DIDN'T CHANGE WHAT I WAS FEELING BUT IT DID CHANGE MY ABILITY TO HIDE IT FROM HIM.

FEELINGS OF OVERWHELM OR INADEQUACY ARE TERRIBLE BUT WHEN YOU

ADD ALL THE THINGS PEOPLE SAY ON TOP:

"IT GOES SO QUICKLY!"

"ENJOY THIS SPECIAL TIME!"

"IT'S SO MAGICAL!"

YOU CAN REALLY FEEL LIKE A FUCKING MONSTER.

YOU'D HAVE TO BE A FUCKING MONSTER TO BE MISERABLE RIGHT NOW.

I MEAN, LOOK AT HER!

SHE'S THE MOST BEAUTIFUL.
SHE'S A CHERUB
SHE'S AN ALIEN

SHE'S A . . .
CRICKET?

I MEAN, IT'S DARK
IN HERE AND MY FACE
HURTS FROM CRYING
BUT I AM ALMOST CERTAIN
MY BABY LOOKS
EXACTLY LIKE
JIMINY CRICKET.

PERFECT BIG EYES,
CARTOON CHEEKS,
& WOULD LOOK FUCKIN' INCREDIBLE IN A TOP HAT.

THE DAY BEFORE I HAD SEEN A LADYBUG IN THE SHOWER.
I AM JUST BARELY WOO-WOO ENOUGH TO ALWAYS RESEARCH THE SPIRITUAL SIGNIFICANCE OF ENCOUNTERS WITH BUGS AND ANIMALS.

THE LADYBUG WAS THERE TO TELL ME "A POSITIVE CHANGE IS COMING"

THE SPIDER IN MY ROOM WAS THERE TO REMIND ME OF "THE POWER OF MY CREATIVITY & FEMININITY"

BUT MY CRICKET-
MY GORGEOUS BABY WHO
APPEARED OUT OF THE
BLUE BUT SOMEHOW EXACTLY
ON TIME—

MY CRICKET IS HERE TO
TELL ME TO "HAVE COURAGE
IN ALL THINGS."

MY CRICKET IS MY REMINDER
ALONG THE PATH THAT
ANYTHING IS POSSIBLE.

AND FOR THE FIRST TIME
SINCE COMING HOME FROM
THE HOSPITAL,

I HAVE A TINY
AMOUNT OF COURAGE

NOT BORROWED OR FAKE.

BUT THE REAL KIND THAT CAN ONLY BE FOUND IN THE DARKNESS AT 3 A.M. AFTER SAYING IT ALL FELT IMPOSSIBLE & YOU MEANT IT

THAT SMALL AMOUNT OF COURAGE HAD MORE IMPACT ON ME THAN ANY PIECE OF ADVICE, NUGGET OF WISDOM, PODCAST, OR BOOK EVER DID

I HELD IT TIGHTLY WHILE I HELD MY BABY. IT GREW A TINY BIT EACH DAY AS SHE DID.

EVERY DAY & EVERY NIGHT MY NEW LIFE BECAME A TINY BIT MORE POSSIBLE.

IT TURNS OUT, I AM NOT A FUCKING MONSTER.

THERE IS NOTHING WRONG WITH ME.

POSTPARTUM IS JUST IMPOSSIBLY HARD.

I CAN'T BELIEVE I DID IT.

I AM SO PROUD OF MYSELF

I HOPE THAT WHEN
YOUR NEW LIFE FEELS
IMPOSSIBLE
YOU CAN FIND A TINY
AMOUNT OF COURAGE.

IT'S PROBABLY CRICKET SIZED
HIDING SOMEWHERE IN
YOUR HOUSE AT 3 A.M.
OR ON A WINDOWSILL
QUIETLY HUMMING
"WHEN YOU WISH UPON
A STAR"

AND UNTIL YOU FIND IT,

IT'S NOT YOUR JOB TO PRETEND LIKE YOU ARE OK IF YOU ARE NOT

IT *IS* YOUR JOB TO FREE YOURSELF FROM THE IDEA THAT YOU ARE FUCKING THIS UP SOMEHOW SO YOU CAN KEEP GOING.

BECAUSE, AS IT TURNS OUT, POSTPARTUM IS IMPOSSIBLY HARD.

I CAN'T BELIEVE YOU'RE DOING IT.

I'M SO PROUD OF YOU.

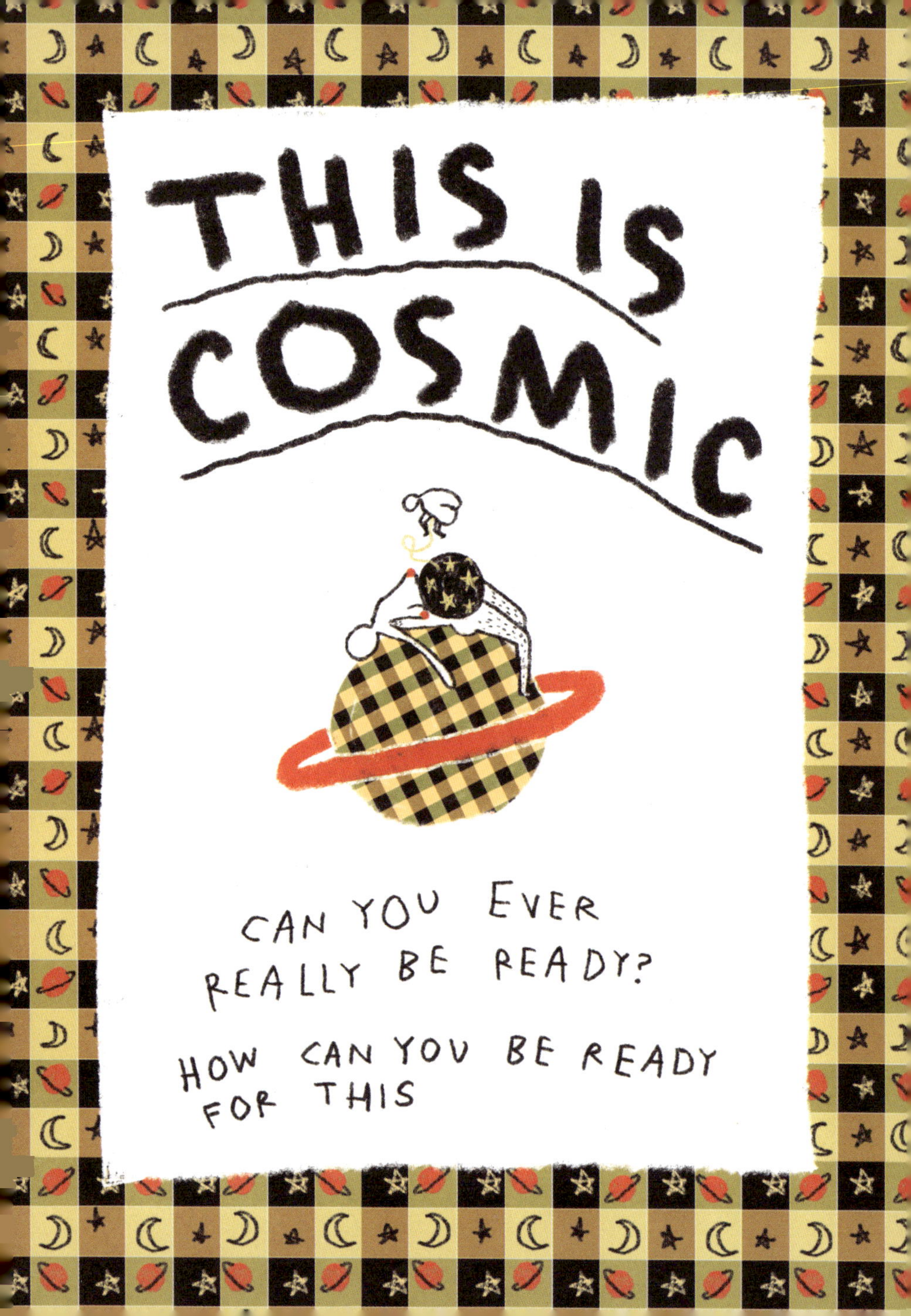
THIS IS
COSMIC
CAN YOU EVER
REALLY BE READY?
HOW CAN YOU BE READY
FOR THIS

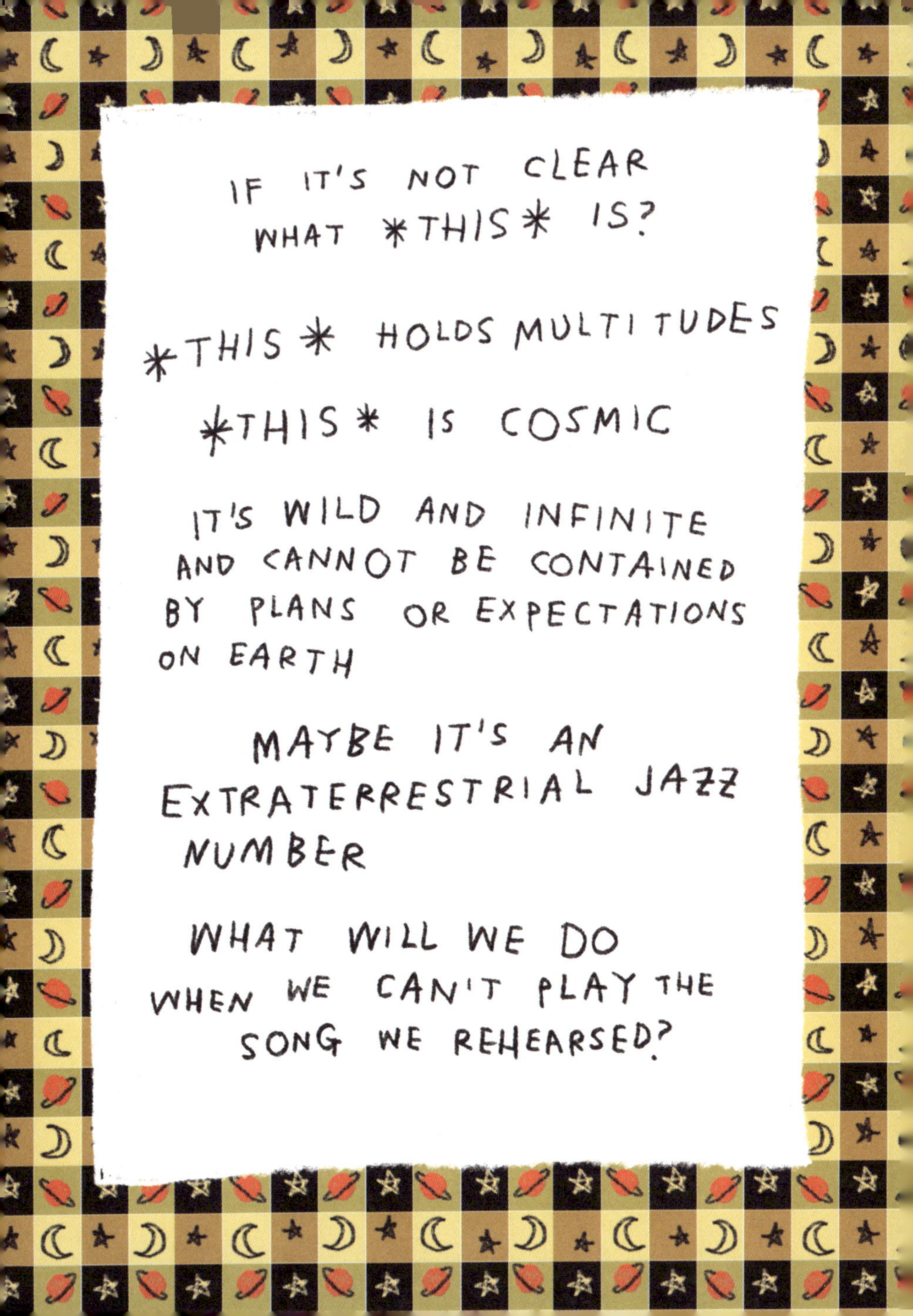
IF IT'S NOT CLEAR
WHAT *THIS* IS?
THIS HOLDS MULTITUDES
THIS IS COSMIC
IT'S WILD AND INFINITE
AND CANNOT BE CONTAINED
BY PLANS OR EXPECTATIONS
ON EARTH
MAYBE IT'S AN
EXTRATERRESTRIAL JAZZ
NUMBER
WHAT WILL WE DO
WHEN WE CAN'T PLAY THE
SONG WE REHEARSED?

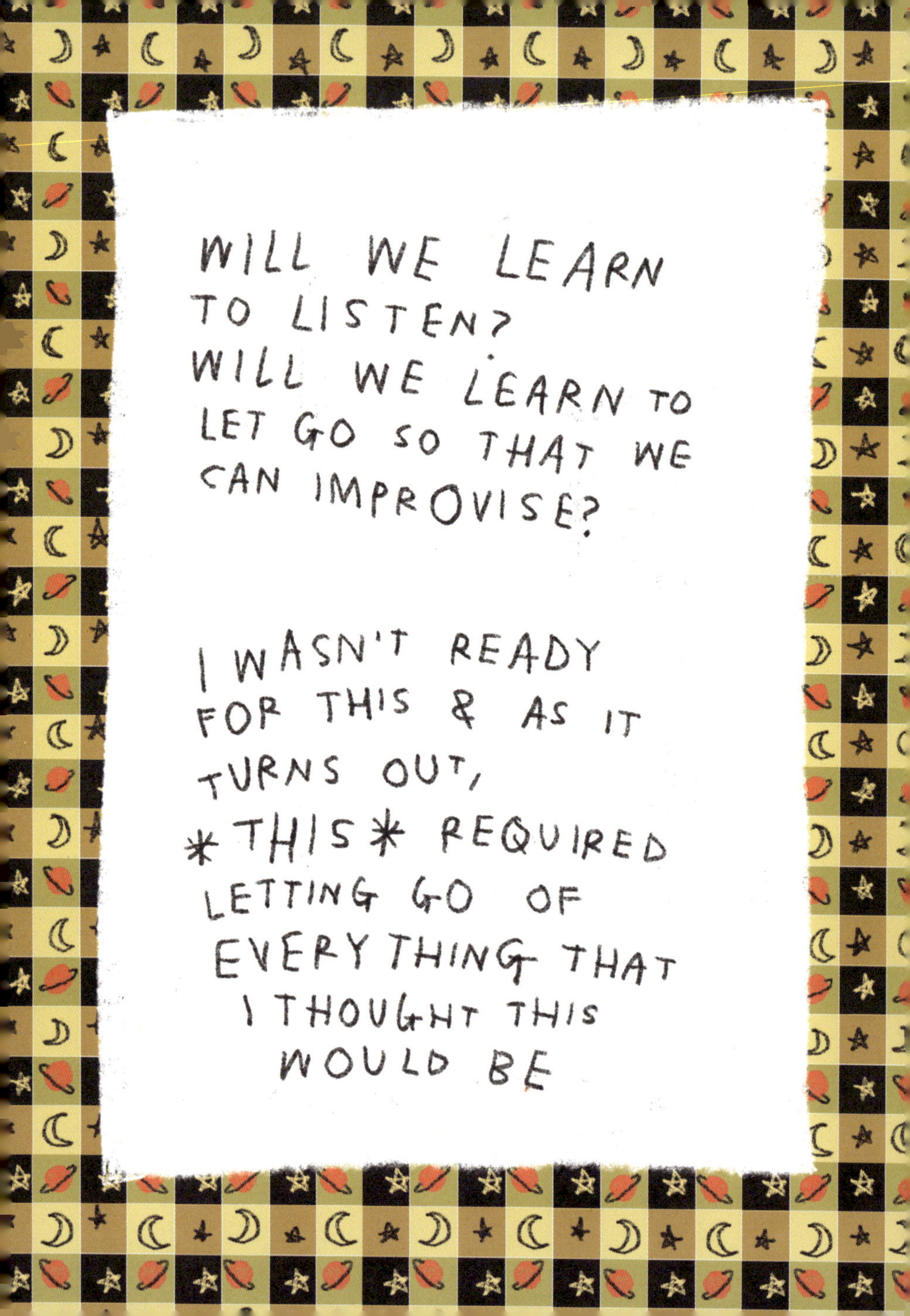
WILL WE LEARN
TO LISTEN?
WILL WE LEARN TO
LET GO SO THAT WE
CAN IMPROVISE?
I WASN'T READY
FOR THIS & AS IT
TURNS OUT,
THIS REQUIRED
LETTING GO OF
EVERYTHING THAT
I THOUGHT THIS
WOULD BE

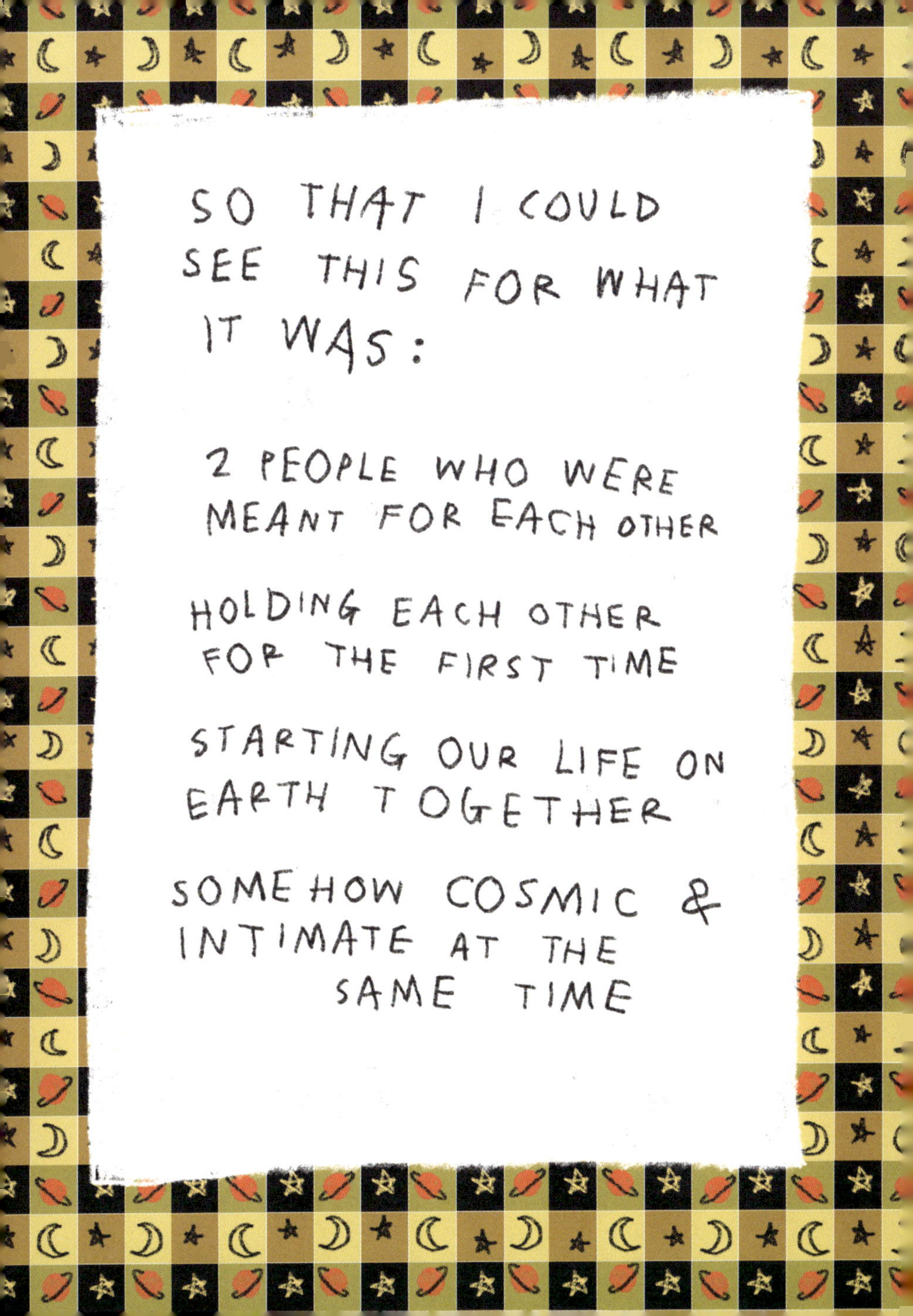
SO THAT I COULD
SEE THIS FOR WHAT
IT WAS:
2 PEOPLE WHO WERE
MEANT FOR EACH OTHER
HOLDING EACH OTHER
FOR THE FIRST TIME
STARTING OUR LIFE ON
EARTH TOGETHER
SOMEHOW COSMIC &
INTIMATE AT THE
SAME TIME

WHEN NOTHING GOES ACCORDING TO PLAN,
IS IT A CURSE?
OR A BLESSING FROM THE COSMOS?
I BELIEVE IT'S A BLESSING, AN OFFERING OF TRUTH
AND IS THERE ANYTHING TRUER THAN WATCHING ALL OF YOUR RIGID EXPECTATIONS

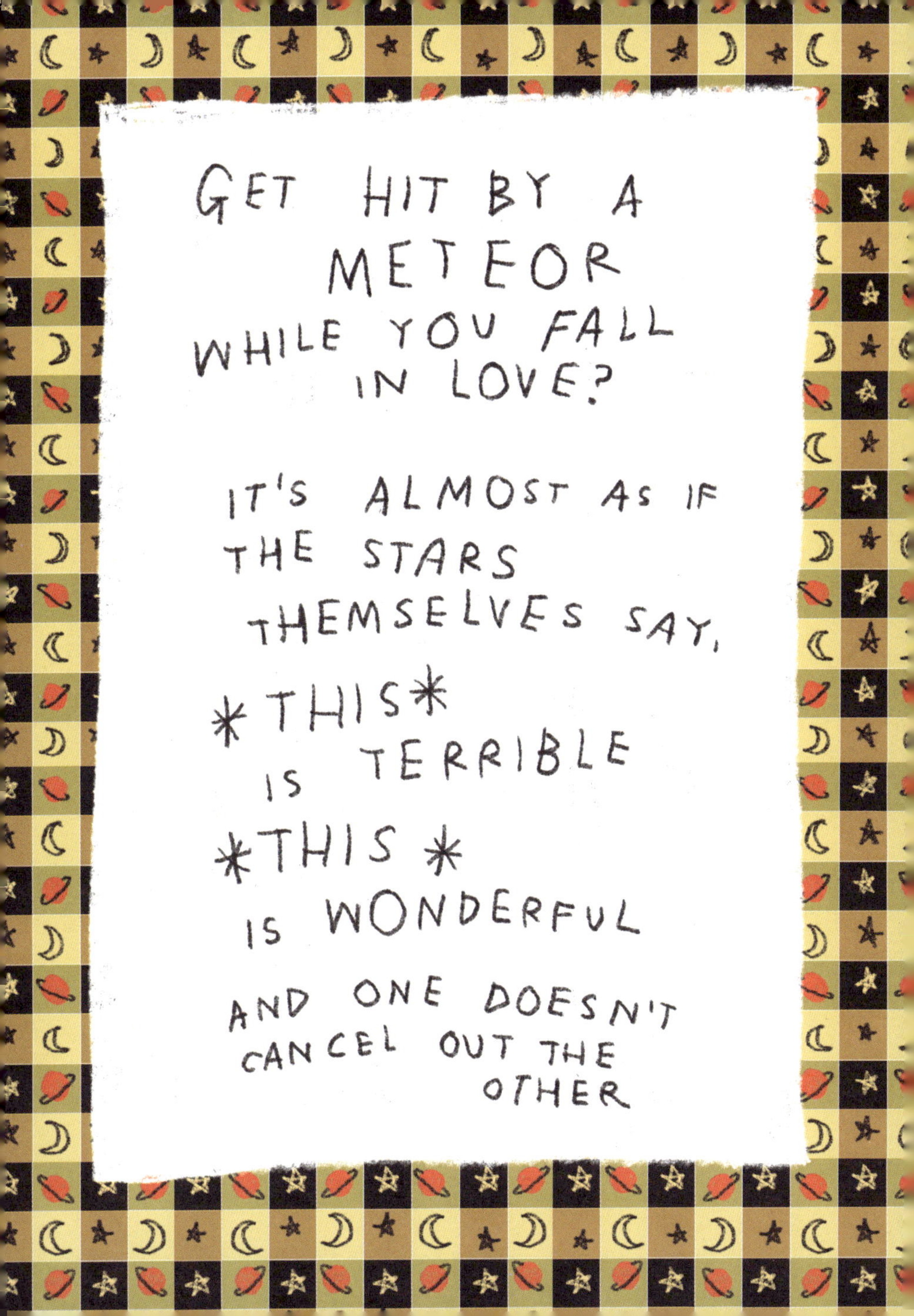
GET HIT BY A
METEOR
WHILE YOU FALL
IN LOVE?
IT'S ALMOST AS IF
THE STARS
THEMSELVES SAY,
THIS
IS TERRIBLE
THIS
IS WONDERFUL
AND ONE DOESN'T
CANCEL OUT THE
OTHER

LEAVING THE HOUSE FEELS EITHER AWKWARD OR IMPOSSIBLE
DEPENDING ON THE DAY
IT FEELS LIKE GOING TO THE CITY FOR THE VERY FIRST TIME

TIME TRAVEL

SOCIAL MEDIA POST

TRAVELING BACK IN TIME TO MAKE A SOCIAL MEDIA POST ABOUT THE BIRTH OF MY CHILD THAT IS

TRUE ♥

RANIBAN IT IS WITH RAW GRATITUDE THAT I ANNOUNCE THAT MY DAUGHTER IS EARTHSIDE AND HEALTHY.
SHE WAS BORN ON A COLD AND CLOUDY MONDAY MORNING

IN NOVEMBER VIA EMERGENCY C-SECTION. THE SURGERY WAS DIFFICULT AND SCARY AND I DIDN'T KNOW, FOR WHAT FELT LIKE AN ETERNITY, IF SHE WAS GOING TO BE OK OR NOT. SHE'S OK AND I'M OK BUT IT FEELS LIKE MY BODY DOESN'T KNOW THAT YET. I FEEL A LACK OF CLOSURE IN MY BIRTH STORY—I DON'T KNOW HOW TO GRIEVE THE LABOR THAT I WANTED TO HAVE WHILE HONORING WHAT I ACTUALLY HAD. WHAT I ACTUALLY HAD WAS AN O.R. FULL OF ANGELS IN SCRUBS. THEY USED EVERY HARD-EARNED SKILL AND INSIGHT TO KEEP MY

LITTLE FAMILY SAFE AND TOGETHER. I TRULY FELT SAFE WITH THEM. MY BOYFRIEND AND MY DAUGHTER WERE MOVED INTO OUR RECOVERY ROOM WHILE THEY STITCHED ME UP. WE GABBED IN THE O.R. LIKE IT WAS A GIRLS' WEEKEND AT A WINERY. I FELT EXHAUSTED AND DRUNK AND IT'S EASY TO LET YOUR GUARD DOWN WHEN ALL YOUR GUARDIAN ANGELS / NEW BESTIES HAVE SEEN ALL YOUR ORGANS ON DISPLAY AND CLEANED YOU UP AFTER YOU GOT POOPED ON WHILE MEETING YOUR DAUGHTER FOR THE VERY FIRST

TIME. WE LAUGHED ABOUT THE POOP AND I TOLD THEM ABOUT MY MOM AND MY SISTER. A WARM SOUTHERN BELLE AND A GUTSY COWGIRL WHOSE LOVE FOR ME (AND ANXIETY LOL) IS SO BIG THAT I COULD FEEL THEM THERE WITH ME.

WHEN THEY ROLLED ME INTO THE RECOVERY ROOM I SAW MY BOYFRIEND STANDING THERE HOLDING OUR DAUGHTER BY THE WINDOW. SHE WAS SLEEPING AND HE WAS SMILING. I COULD SEE THE WORLD OUTSIDE THE WINDOW AND A FAMILIAR PANIC SET IN. WHAT WAS I THINKING?

HOW COULD I BRING HER INTO A WORLD THAT IS SO FUCKED UP? BUT THEN AN EXHALE. MY LITTLE GIRL HAS MY BOYFRIEND AS HER DAD.

HE HELD MY HAND SO TIGHT DURING SURGERY THAT DAY, AS IF TRYING TO SQUEEZE OUT ANY POSSIBILITY THAT I COULD FEEL ALONE. HE HELD MY HAND THAT WAY AS WE WALKED SIDE BY SIDE THROUGH PARIS, LONDON, AND BARCELONA WHEN WE WERE 21. I HAVE ALWAYS FELT SAFE AND FREE WITH HIM, WORDS I THOUGHT WERE OPPOSITES BUT HE HAS SHOWN ME THAT THEY'RE NOT.

I PICTURED HIM HOLDING HER HAND WHILE HE SHOWED HER PARIS, LONDON, AND BARCELONA. I WAS LIVING PROOF THAT WITH HER DAD, SHE WOULD ALWAYS BE BOTH SAFE AND FREE, NO POSSIBILITY OF FEELING ALONE.

THIS IS THE PART WHERE I AM SUPPOSED TO TELL YOU HER FULL LEGAL NAME, HOW MANY INCHES SHE WAS AT BIRTH, AND HOW MUCH SHE WEIGHED. BUT I AM NOT GOING TO DO THAT BECAUSE ... I FIND SHARING THAT INFO TO BE SO STRANGE. IT HAS STATE-FAIR LIVESTOCK ENERGY.

I CALL HER CRICKET AND SHE WAS, LIKE ALL BABIES, BABY SIZED.

I FEEL LIKE I SHOULD SHARE SOME JOY AND WONDER, MAYBE SAY SOMETHING LIKE, "YOU ARE SO LOVED, *ENTER ENTIRE LEGAL NAME HERE*! SO EXCITED TO START OUR LIFE AS A FAMILY OF 3." SHE IS SO LOVED AND OF COURSE I AM EXCITED, IN THEORY, ABOUT OUR NEW LIFE. BUT IF I CLOSED WITH THAT, I'D BE DOING IT BECAUSE I THINK IT'S WHAT YOU WANT TO HEAR. SO, INSTEAD I'LL LEAVE YOU WITH THIS:

I STARTED SEEING A POSTPARTUM THERAPIST 5 DAYS AFTER SHE WAS BORN. RIGHT BEFORE LEAVING THE HOSPITAL, ONE OF THE ANGELS IN SCRUBS WHISPERED TO ME:

"IF YOU FEEL SAD OR SCARED WHEN YOU'RE HOME, CALL US IMMEDIATELY OR SAY IT TO SOMEONE YOU TRUST."

I FELT INCREDIBLY SAD AND SCARED A COUPLE DAYS LATER. IF I DIDN'T LEAVE THE HOSPITAL WITH THOSE WORDS, I DON'T KNOW HOW LONG IT WOULD HAVE TAKEN FOR ME TO ASK FOR THE HELP THAT I NEEDED TO SORT THROUGH THE FEELINGS THAT I THOUGHT MADE ME A BAD MOM FOR HAVING IN THE FIRST PLACE. I WAS NOT A BAD MOM, I HAD POSTPARTUM DEPRESSION.

SO HERE'S TO ASKING FOR HELP, TO MY STITCHED-UP BODY, TO THE ANGELS IN SCRUBS, AND TO MY BOYFRIEND.

AND HERE'S TO MY DAUGHTER WHO WAS BORN ON A DAY WITH CLOUDS SO BIG AND SO DARK THEY LOOKED LIKE THEY COULD BURST AT ANY MOMENT.

BUT THE CLOUDS HELD IT ALL IN UNTIL SHE WAS BORN THEN THERE WAS THUNDER AND A RELEASE. THE CLOUDS CRIED AND SO DID I.

SHE'S FINALLY HERE, MY DAUGHTER
WHO WAS BORN WITH, YES,
THE STRENGTH
AND
TENACITY OF
WINTER,
BUT MOST OF ALL,
THE
HOPE
OF
SPRING.

I AM MY FAVORITE PERSON'S FAVORITE PERSON

YOU UNAMBIGUOUSLY
LOVE ME
AND NOT A TYPE OF LOVE
THAT TAKES INTO ACCOUNT
HOW I LOOK
OR
WHAT I'VE ACCOMPLISHED
OR
WHAT I CAN PROVIDE

BUT A TYPE OF LOVE
THAT NEEDS ME TO ___BE___
NOTHING ELSE,
JUST BE HERE.
AND IN THIS MOMENT,
BEING LOVED IN THIS WAY
FEELS LIKE FREEDOM.

IT FREES ME
FROM ALL THE BULLSHIT
THE WORLD HAS TOLD ME
ABOUT WHY
I MATTER

PART 1: TL;DR

CAN YOU EVER REALLY BE READY? I WASN'T READY. I GENERALLY DO NOT KNOW WHAT I AM DOING IN LIFE BUT I DO KNOW THAT WE WERE MEANT TO BE TOGETHER. IT FEELS COSMIC BUT DEEPLY INTIMATE AT THE SAME TIME.

BABIES DO NOT GIVE A SHIT ABOUT OUR PLANS. MAYBE POSTPARTUM IS A JAZZ NUMBER. WHAT WILL WE DO WHEN WE

CAN'T PLAY THE SONG WE REHEARSED?

WILL WE LET GO AND IMPROVISE?

A QUICK NOTE FROM THE FUTURE: 2 THINGS CAN BE TRUE AT THE SAME TIME! THIS IS TERRIBLE AND THIS IS WONDERFUL, AND ONE DOESN'T CANCEL OUT THE OTHER.

BEING LOVED THIS WAY FEELS LIKE FREEDOM. IT FREES ME FROM ALL THE BULLSHIT THE WORLD HAS TOLD ME ABOUT WHY I MATTER.

PART 2: EARTH GARDEN

AND ALL OF A SUDDEN, MY FEET WERE BACK ON THE GROUND.

WOULD I MISS FLOATING IN THE COSMOS?

YES, IT WAS LONELY UP THERE, BUT IT WAS ETHEREAL. THERE WAS A BLURRY GLOW THAT COVERED EVERYTHING.

I WAS TOO FAR FROM EARTH TO MAKE OUT ANY OF THE DETAILS. I COULD EXIST AS I WAS: A STRANGE, COSMIC, AMORPHOUS HUMANLIKE MATERNAL CREATURE.

I DIDN'T FIND ANY OF IT EASY, ALL OF IT FELT AWKWARD, BUT BY DOING IT ANYWAY OUT THERE AMONG THE STARS, I LEARNED THAT I WAS CAPABLE.

BUT BEING BACK ON EARTH HAS ME SECOND-GUESSING ALL OF MY NEW AND HARD-WON CAPABILITIES.

ALL EARTH-DWELLING MOMS SEEM TO HAVE <u>EVERYTHING</u> FIGURED OUT SOMEHOW? THEY LOOK LIKE HAVING A BABY DIDN'T CATAPULT THEM BEYOND THE EARTH'S SOLAR SYSTEM AND INTO THE DARK UNKNOWN. THEY SEEM FINE... HOW ARE THEY FINE? *ARE* THEY FINE??

BEING BACK ON EARTH HAS TURNED ALL OF MY MATERNAL CREATURE INSTINCTS INTO INVITATIONS TO BE TOLD EITHER DIRECTLY OR INDIRECTLY THAT MY MATERNAL INSTINCTS ARE WRONG, I AM WRONG.

SO YES, OUT IN SPACE, I LEARNED THAT I CAN DO THIS, BUT NOW I MUST FIGURE OUT HOW ON EARTH I WANT TO DO THIS, NO MATTER THE CHATTER.

ONLY I CAN ANSWER~

IS MY RIGHT BOOB
TRYING TO TELL ME
SOMETHING?

AM I A DAYCARE PARENT?
WILL IT BREAK ME TO HAND
MY BABY TO A STRANGER?
WILL IT BREAK ME IF I DON'T?

WILL IT RUIN MY BABY
IF I DO SLEEP TRAINING?
WILL IT RUIN ME IF
I DON'T?

WILL I EVER PAINT AGAIN?
WILL I EVER WRITE AGAIN?

WHY WON'T I GIVE MYSELF PERMISSION TO HATE BREASTFEEDING?
WHY DO I HATE BREASTFEEDING?

AND,
HOW DO I KEEP MY EARTH GARDEN WATERED WITH A BABY IN MY ARMS?

I WAS TOLD THIS WOULD STABILIZE ME
THAT IT WOULD GIVE ME PURPOSE
MAKE ME LESS RESTLESS
MAKE ME FEEL LESS LOST
I WAS TOLD THIS WOULD STABILIZE ME
BUT I AM COMPLETELY
AND THOROUGHLY
DESTABILIZED

I HAVEN'T FELT THIS SINCE I WAS 13
IS THIS PUBERTY AGAIN?
I HAVE 100 NEW DESIRES
AND NO WORDS TO DESCRIBE ANY
OF THEM
I HAVE A BODY THAT
DOESN'T FEEL LIKE MINE
AND NO IDEA
HOW TO CARE FOR IT
OR DRESS IT
OR LIVE IN IT

I HAVE HEIGHTENED
FEELINGS

ELECTRIC SENSATIONS

AND AN ACUTE SENSE
THAT NO ONE WILL
UNDERSTAND THEM

WILL THEY BE WORRIED
ABOUT ME IF I TELL THEM
THAT THE ONLY WAY FOR ME
TO FEEL OK
IS TO ROLLERSKATE NAKED
IN THE BASEMENT
PUNCHING THE AIR
TO OLIVIA RODRIGO'S
SONG "BRUTAL"

AM I ALLOWED TO SCREAM

AND YELL

THIS IS REALLY WEIRD

WHILE POINTING FRANTICALLY AT ... EVERYTHING?

WOULD IT BE UNSETTLING IF I JUST CAME OUT AND SAID IT:

I AM A TIME TRAVELER AND YOU NEED TO HELP ME TRAVEL BACK

BECAUSE I SKIPPED THE PART OF MY LIFE THAT WOULD TEACH ME HOW TO BE A MOM ON PLANET EARTH AND... I THINK EVERYONE CAN TELL AND I FEEL ASHAMED.

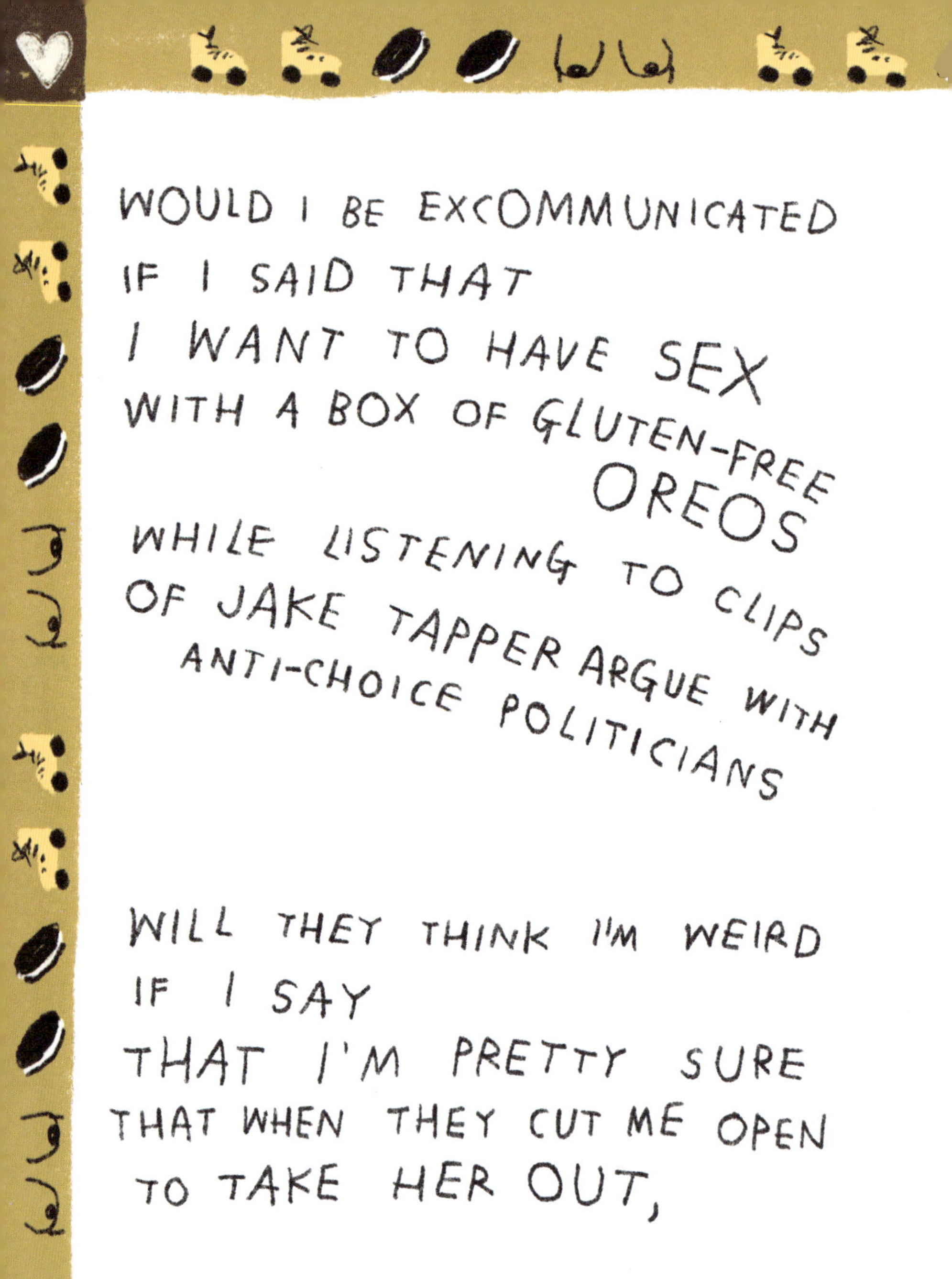
WOULD I BE EXCOMMUNICATED
IF I SAID THAT
I WANT TO HAVE SEX
WITH A BOX OF GLUTEN-FREE
OREOS
WHILE LISTENING TO CLIPS
OF JAKE TAPPER ARGUE WITH
ANTI-CHOICE POLITICIANS
WILL THEY THINK I'M WEIRD
IF I SAY
THAT I'M PRETTY SURE
THAT WHEN THEY CUT ME OPEN
TO TAKE HER OUT,

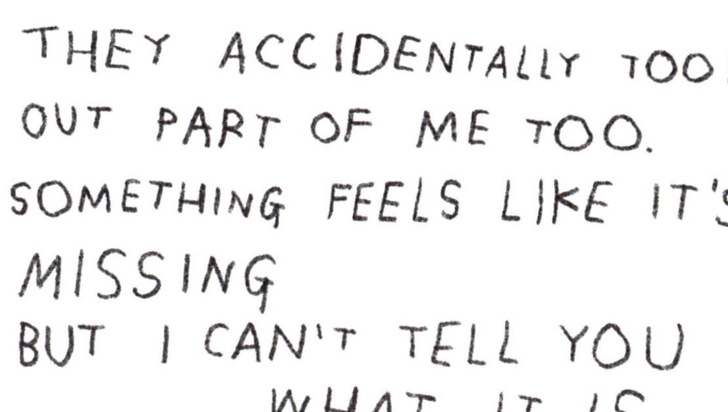

THEY ACCIDENTALLY TOOK
OUT PART OF ME TOO.
SOMETHING FEELS LIKE IT'S
MISSING
BUT I CAN'T TELL YOU
WHAT IT IS

IS IT OK TO SAY OUT LOUD
THAT BIRTH WAS SCARY & BAD

AND THE FLASHBACKS
WON'T STOP

I SEE IT ALL AGAIN,
BUT MY BRAIN REWRITES
THE ENDING AND IT'S SAD

AM I ALLOWED TO SAY
SORRY, I CAN'T TALK TODAY,
I NEED SOME TIME BECAUSE
YESTERDAY I FELT LIKE A GODDESS
IN THE SUN
AND TODAY I FEEL LIKE A GOBLIN,
AND I DON'T KNOW
WHICH IS TRUE.
IS THERE SPACE FOR ME
AS I AM?

ALL THE PARTS OF ME
(NAKED SKATER, CONFUSED,
TIME TRAVELER, WEIRD & HORNY,
MISSING PARTS, STUCK IN A
LOOP, 1/2 GODDESS 1/2 GOBLIN)
ARE THEY ALLOWED TO BE
HERE NOW THAT I'M A MOM?

AND THEN ONE AFTERNOON
AS I'M USING A CONTRAPTION
TO SUCK MUCUS OUT OF
MY BABY'S NOSE AND A FEW
DROPS OF MILK FALL OUT
OF MY LEFT BOOB
IT BECOMES SUDDENLY CLEAR

I REALLY NEED TO STOP
THINKING ABOUT WHAT OTHER
PEOPLE THINK BECAUSE THIS!

THIS IS A REALLY WEIRD
PHASE IN MY LIFE

AND I CAN DO WEIRD.

I CRIED A TEAR FOR MY PAST SELF. DOES SHE THINK I FORGOT HER? I HOPE SHE FORGIVES ME FOR LEAVING HER BEHIND WHEN I WENT INTO THE O.R. FOR MY C-SECTION.

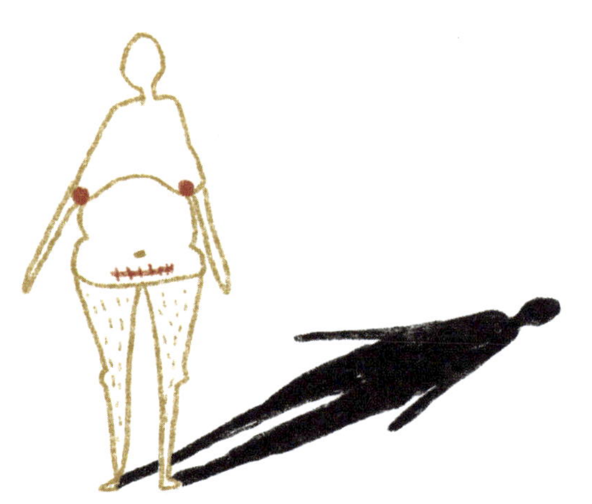

SHE SHOWED UP TODAY
WHEN I TURNED ON MY
'80s PLAYLIST.

I WAS NERVOUS.

BUT SHE TOLD ME SHE WAS
PROUD OF ME WHILE
SHE HELD MY SCAR
AND I CRIED
FROM EVERYWHERE.

DAFFODILS, FORSYTHIA, & DANDELIONS

EARLY SPRING AND THE
WORLD IS BROWN AND GREY

EVERYTHING IS MUDDY AND TIRED
AND I AM TOO

I AM HIDING MYSELF AWAY
FEELING SELF-CONSCIOUS

ABOUT THE WAYS THAT I'VE
CHANGED OVER WINTER.
WHAT WILL THEY THINK OF ME?
OF MY NEW BODY AND MY
NEW LIFE?
BUT THEN ONE GREY DAY
I STEP OUTSIDE AND SEE
THE DAFFODILS ARE
JUMPING OUT OF THE SOIL
LIKE BISCUITS OUT OF A CAN

AND FORSYTHIA LIKE FIREWORKS
SET OFF ON THE SIDE OF THE ROAD
AND THE DANDELIONS
POPPING OUT OF THE GRASS
LIKE POPCORN ON THE STOVE
NONE OF THE OTHERS ARE
READY YET, THEY'RE ALL
HIDING AWAY

THE LILIES ARE STILL RESTING;
THEY STOOD SO TALL ALL
SUMMER IN HIGH HEELS AND
THEIR FEET ARE TIRED.

THE IRISES ARE TOO
SENSITIVE FOR THIS MOODY
WEATHER.

AND THE TULIPS,
WELL, THEY HAVE HAD NPR
ON ALL WINTER AND GIVEN
THE CURRENT STATE OF THE WORLD
ARE HOSTING A TOWN HALL
TO VOTE ON WHETHER TO
COME UP AT ALL

BUT THE DAFFODILS,
FORSYTHIA,
AND DANDELIONS

THEY DON'T CARE ABOUT
WHAT OTHERS THINK

THEY DON'T REQUIRE
A MAJORITY VOTE

THEY AREN'T LOOKING
IN THE MIRROR TO SEE
IF THEY LOOK THE SAME
AS LAST SPRING

THEY'RE USING ALL THEIR
ENERGY
TO FIND THE SUN

THEY EXPAND
AND STRETCH
AND GROW

BECAUSE THEY KNOW
LIVING THINGS
AREN'T SUPPOSED
TO STAY
THE SAME

OH
THE
ABUNDANCE
I DIDN'T
KNOW I HAD
INSIDE OF
ME

SNAKES

IN AN UNEXPECTED TURN OF EVENTS, I—A MUSEUM/THRIFT STORE/BOOKSTORE/INSIDE PERSON—FELL IN LOVE WITH KEEPING A GARDEN. I AM NOT GOOD AT IT. THINK THE OPPOSITE OF MARTHA STEWART. PICTURE ME POLKA-DOTTED WITH MOSQUITO BITES AND WEARING ONE OF THOSE SUN HATS WITH A NECK FLAP. MY CROCS ARE FILLED WITH DIRT AND I'M YELLING AT MY PIT BULL, TONY, BECAUSE HE JUMPED INTO A TOMATO PLANT.

I LOVE MY CHAOTIC GARDEN AND IT LOVES ME BACK. IT MAKES MY MIND QUIET (A MIRACLE) AND FILLS MY ARMS WITH COLORFUL THINGS THAT I GET TO SHARE WITH THE PEOPLE I LOVE.

SO WHEN CRICKET CAME ALONG, THIS NEW PERSON I LOVE THE MOST, I COULDN'T WAIT TO SHARE THE GARDEN WITH HER. I PICTURED US OUT THERE AT DUSK, TOY TRACTORS AND DINOSAURS AMONG THE VEGGIES, WAITING FOR FIREFLIES WHILE WE FILLED OUR POCKETS WITH LITTLE ORANGE TOMATOES.

AND SO WHEN THE DAYS GOT LONGER AND CRICKET AND I GOT STRONGER, I FASTENED MY NECK FLAP HAT UNDER MY CHIN, THEN FASTENED HER TINY NECK FLAP HAT UNDER HERS, AND INTRODUCED HER TO MY GARDEN.

I PRACTICED TENDING TO HER AND TO THE GARDEN AT THE SAME TIME & WE GOT THE HANG OF IT!

THEN ONE DAY, WHILE PICKING YELLOW SQUASH, HATS FASTENED, CROCS ON, AND CRICKET STRAPPED TO MY BACK, I SAW A SNAKE. A REALLY FUCKING BIG SHIMMERY BLACK SNAKE. I THINK MY BUTTHOLE ACTUALLY FELL OUT OF MY PANTS AND THEN I RAN INSIDE ON MY TIPTOES FOR SOME REASON. I COULDN'T CATCH MY BREATH.

GOD, I HATE SNAKES SO MUCH. I WON'T EVEN WALK PAST THE SNAKES AT THE BRONX ZOO. NOW THAT CRICKET IS HERE, I HAVE THIS VERY UNHINGED BUFFY-THE-VAMPIRE-SLAYER ENERGY TOWARD ANYTHING THAT COULD POSE A THREAT TO HER. AND SURE, ALL CREDIBLE SOURCES SAID THAT THIS PARTICULAR SNAKE IS "NOT POISONOUS" BUT I AM NO FOOL. I SAW IT WITH MY OWN EYES AND IT HAD BIG POISON ENERGY.

IN THE DAYS THAT FOLLOWED, I COULD NOT SHAKE IT. I WAS ON HIGH ALERT AT ALL TIMES. I WOULD BUFFY BACKFLIP YOUR ASS IF YOU MADE ANY SUDDEN MOVES. INTELLECTUALLY I UNDERSTOOD THAT THERE WERE ALWAYS SNAKES IN MY GARDEN BECAUSE SNAKES LIVE OUTSIDE AND MY GARDEN IS ALSO OUTSIDE. BUT REASONING WITH MY ACTIVATED NERVOUS SYSTEM WAS A NO-GO AND I JUST DECIDED, FINE! IT'S NO PROBLEM! I WILL JUST NOT GO OUTSIDE! I WAS ALWAYS AN INSIDE PERSON ANYWAYS. I AM RETURNING FROM WHENCE I CAME.

FOR A WEEK I FOUGHT WITH MYSELF. MY BRAIN WOULD START SOMETHING WITH MY NERVOUS SYSTEM, CALL HER A "TINY LITTLE BITCH" OR SOMETHING. MY NERVOUS SYSTEM WOULD SNAP BACK AND SAY... "ANY ADULT PERSON WHO THINKS IT'S OK TO SEND A *BABY* INTO A FUCKIN' SNAKE LAIR HELL PIT IS STUPID AND ALSO EVIL"

(SHOUT-OUT TO ME FOR THINKING MY ONLY OPTIONS WERE TINY LITTLE BITCH OR EVIL PERSON.)

THEN ONE DAY I ANNOUNCED TO NOBODY: I AM GOING BACK OUT! CUE ELTON JOHN BECAUSE THIS BITCH HAS FOUND HER PLACE ON THE PATH UNWINDING.

I STRAPPED CRICKET ON MY BACK AND THREW THE BACK DOOR OPEN. THE FRESH AIR!!!!! THE BIRDS!!!!! I MADE IT EXACTLY 4 STEPS BEFORE I SAW MY BLACK GARDEN HOSE COILED UP EXACTLY WHERE IT'S ALWAYS BEEN, FREAKED OUT, AND RAN BACK INSIDE.

WHY COULDN'T I PULL MYSELF TOGETHER? THAT HOSE IS DEFINITELY NOT A SNAKE AND THERE HAD ALWAYS BEEN DANGER EVERYWHERE. WILLINGLY SHOWING UP IN A DANGEROUS WORLD WAS POSSIBLE WHEN IT WAS JUST ME.

BUT WHEN CRICKET SHOWED UP, SHE PRIED MY HEART WIDE OPEN. SO OPEN I CAN HEAR IT WHISTLE WHEN THE WIND BLOWS.

HOW IS ANYONE SUPPOSED TO LIVE LIKE THIS? WITH A WIDE-OPEN HEART AND DANGER EVERYWHERE?

CAN I USE THIS NEWFOUND BUFFY-WITH-A-WOODEN-STAKE ENERGY TO HOPE & FIGHT FOR GOOD IN HER LIFE INSTEAD OF ANTICIPATING DANGER AT EVERY TURN?

TODAY I FELT AFRAID AND MY HEART FELT TENDER BUT I TOOK HER OUTSIDE ANYWAYS. WE CAME BACK INSIDE WITH DIRT ON OUR FACES AND LITTLE TOMATOES IN OUR POCKETS.

WE DIDN'T SEE ANY SNAKES,

BUT WE DID SEE

A MONARCH BUTTERFLY,
A FAMILY OF DEER,
A HAWK OVERHEAD,
CARDINALS IN THE MAPLE TREE,
A GIANT EARTHWORM,
A MOUSE,
A MALLARD DUCK ON THE POND,
THAT ONE FROG THAT LIVES UNDER THE PATIO THAT I NAMED JEFF FOR SOME REASON,
A GRASSHOPPER,
AND A HONEYBEE.

TODAY I FEEL
WORTHY OF
DAVID ATTENBOROUGH
NARRATION

I AM A BUTTERFLY
A RAINBOW
A SUNFLOWER DROPPING
SEEDS

FROG LANDLINE

EVERYTHING IS CHANGING

THE TOOTHPASTE IS OUT OF THE TUBE~
IT'S NOT GOING BACK

& IT'S NOT THAT I NECESSARILY WANT
IT TO GO BACK IN THE TUBE...

I WANTED THIS BABY

I WANTED THESE CHANGES

I'M JUST TIRED

SO TODAY I AM GOING TO CELEBRATE WHAT HAS STAYED THE SAME

THE STEADFAST, THE ESSENTIAL, THE PARTS OF ME THAT DON'T HAVE TO GROW UP:

☆ DRAWS IN COMPOSITION NOTEBOOKS WITH SHARPIES

☆ ARRANGES FRUIT IN A FRUIT BOWL ROYGBIV

☆ PLAYS DAVID BOWIE IN THE CAR

☆ FRENCH FRIES FOR DINNER

☆ PERFECTLY HAPPY TO SPEND THE DAY ALONE

☆ GENTLY CATCHES A FROG
AND HOLDS IT UP TO MY FACE
GORGEOUS, I WHISPER

TOMORROW I'LL CONTINUE
TO CHANGE

BUT FOR NOW THIS IS NICE~

SAYING HELLO TO THE PARTS OF
ME THAT ARE LEFT UNTOUCHED
BY TIME & THEY WERE JUST AS
I LEFT THEM

IT'S SO SPECIAL
THAT I STILL REALLY LIKE FROGS

BECAUSE CATCHING ONE IN
MY HANDS

IS LIKE A LANDLINE WITH
A CURLY CORD

ATTACHED TO WHERE
I STARTED.

SCATTER-BRAINED

I THOUGHT I WAS SCATTER-BRAINED BEFORE

BUT *THIS*

WELL, THIS IS A TOTA

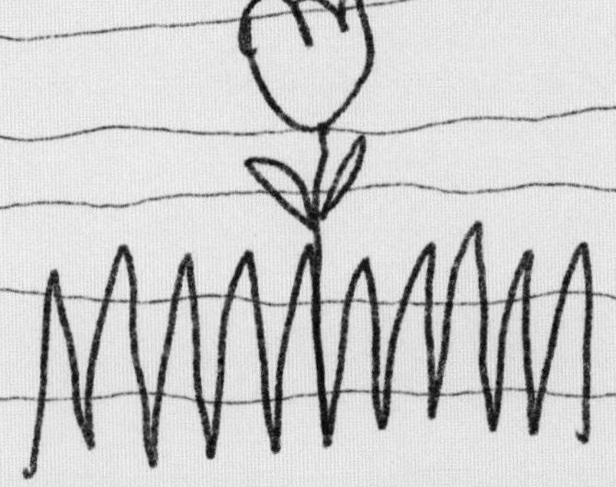

PART 2: TL;DR

I AM A STRANGE, COSMIC, AMORPHOUS HUMANLIKE MATERNAL CREATURE.

HOW DO I KEEP MY EARTH GARDEN WATERED WITH A BABY IN MY ARMS?

IS IT OK TO SAY MY THOUGHTS OUT LOUD IF THEY ARE SCARY OR BAD?

IS THERE SPACE FOR ME AS I AM?

I WANT TO BE EMBRACED, FORGIVEN, AND UNDERSTOOD.

THE FLOWERS IN SPRING WILL SHOW THE WAY.

PART 3:
MYTHOS

HOW DO I RECONCILE THE DICHOTOMY? THERE IS SO MUCH SPACE BETWEEN HOW MY NEW LIFE APPEARS & HOW IT FEELS.

FROM THE OUTSIDE LOOKING IN, THERE IS A WARM GLOW. A COMFORT THAT COMES FROM AN ASSUMED DEVOTION TO A CONVENTIONAL WAY OF LIFE. THERE IS A TRANQUIL, HOMELY, AND COZY AURA THAT SURROUNDS EVERYTHING.

BUT IN TRUTH, I HAVE ENTERED A PORTAL AND ARRIVED IN A LAND SO UNKNOWN TO ME, IT MIGHT AS WELL BE FILLED WITH OGRES AND DRAGONS.

THIS IS A HEROINE'S JOURNEY. UNLIKE THE HERO'S JOURNEY THAT ENDS AFTER EXTERNAL OBSTACLES HAVE BEEN OVERCOME, THIS IS A COMPLEX, MULTISTEP PSYCHOSPIRITUAL JOURNEY. THERE WILL BE DEATHS TO OLD SELVES, AWAKENINGS TO NEW SELVES, OLD WOUNDS THAT REQUIRE HEALING, AND DUALITIES TO INTEGRATE.

HERE I CREATE SPACE FOR
THE PARTS OF THE PROCESS
THAT FELT OTHERWORLDLY.
HOW BEAUTIFUL,
HOW LONELY,
TO BE IN A MYTHICAL
REALM BEHIND CLOSED DOORS.
WELCOME
TO
MINE.

SHEWOLF

I AM STARTING TO REALIZE THAT WHEN I MADE JOKES ABOUT NAMING MY CHILD ROMULUS OR REMUS SO THAT I COULD NAME MYSELF SHEWOLF, I WASN'T JOKING AT ALL. I WAS REALLY ON TO SOMETHING.

I FIRST SAW SHEWOLF WHEN I WAS A 19-YEAR-OLD ART HISTORY STUDENT IN ROME.

MY DAYS WERE SPENT STUDYING ART THAT WAS MADE FOR AND BY MEN. I SAW DOZENS OF SOLDIERS, EMPERORS, PHILOSOPHERS, AND SAINTS WITH STURDY BODIES AND FURROWED BROWS.

... AND THEN I SAW *HER*. AND ONCE I NOTICED HER I STARTED TO SEE HER EVERYWHERE. A GORGEOUS REPRIEVE FROM THE MASCULINE PERSPECTIVES THAT DOMINATED MY TEXTBOOKS AND TOURS. I FOUND HER CARVED IN BRONZE AND MARBLE, PAINTED, AND DEPICTED IN MOSAICS.

SHE BECAME MY ROMAN COMPANION AND MY WISE PROTECTOR AS I WALKED THE CITY ALONE.

HERE IS HOW I REMEMBER HER:
A FIERCE WOLF,
OFTEN SHOWING TEETH AS IF SHE'S SAYING "I DARE YOU TO FUCK WITH ME LOL."
AND BELOW THE SAFE CANOPY OF HER BODY, 2 SOFT AND TINY BABIES, ROMULUS AND REMUS, DRINKING FROM HER BREASTS.

THOSE 2 BABIES' MERE EXISTENCE POSED A THREAT TO THE REIGN OF THEIR UNCLE, KING AMULIUS, SO HE ORDERED THEM TO BE KILLED.

ROMULUS AND REMUS WERE LEFT TO DIE IN THE TIBER RIVER, BUT SHEWOLF PULLED THEM FROM THE RIVER AND NURSED THEM BACK TO LIFE.

IN DOING SO, SHE CHANGED HISTORY INTO A STORY ABOUT WHAT HAPPENS WHEN BABIES ARE RAISED BY WILD (WOLF) MOTHERS. THEY GROW UP TO OVERTHROW THE KING.

THEREIN LIES MY INSPIRATION FOR NAMING MYSELF SHEWOLF. THAT, AND THE NAME *MOM* FEELS AWKWARD WHEN I WEAR IT. SO I RESEARCHED ITS ETYMOLOGY, LOOKING FOR SOMETHING IN THERE THAT WOULD FEEL LIKE ME. BUT THE WORDS *MOTHER*, *MOM*, *MAMA*, *MOMMY*... ARE BORN OUT OF BABY TALK. THEY ARE NAMES INTENDED TO CREATE EASE FOR THE BUBBLY BABY MOUTHS THAT SAY THEM. IT'S SO SIMPLE. IT'S SO DIRECT. SHOULDN'T I FIND THAT BEAUTIFUL?

YET HERE I AM, AIRING MY ETYMOLOGICAL GRIEVANCES. THE NAME "MOM" JUST DOES NOT CAPTURE THE WAY IT FEELS TO INHABIT THAT ROLE.

THE ROLE OF *MOM* I.R.L. & THE ROLE OF WOLVES IN MYTHOLOGY RUN PARALLEL. THEY—WE—ARE WILD, WISE, PROTECTIVE, OFTEN ALONE, NAVIGATING THE DENSE AND TANGLED WOODS, HOWLING AT THE MOON, VOLATILE, LOVING, TENDER, AND FIERCE.

SHEWOLF CAPTURES MY SOFTNESS AND THE PARTS OF ME WITH SHARP TEETH.

SHE IS MY COMPANION, MY WISE PROTECTOR, MY INSPIRATION, AND MY REMINDER THAT SIMPLE CARE TASKS LIKE FEEDING A BABY AREN'T SIMPLE AT ALL. THEY'RE LITERALLY THE FIRST STEP TO OVERTHROW THE KING.

PATRON SAINT
OF MY LIFE
IS A MESS
MY BABA HAS WILD HAIR
AND EYES QUICK TO FILL WITH TEARS
SHE TALKS TO SAINTS OUT LOUD
AS IF THEY'RE IN THE ROOM
SHE USED TO WRITE ME POEMS IN CURSIVE
ON YELLOW LEGAL PAD PAPER
A FEW SINCERE & RHYMING LINES
FOLDED INTO A LITTLE WHITE ENVELOPE

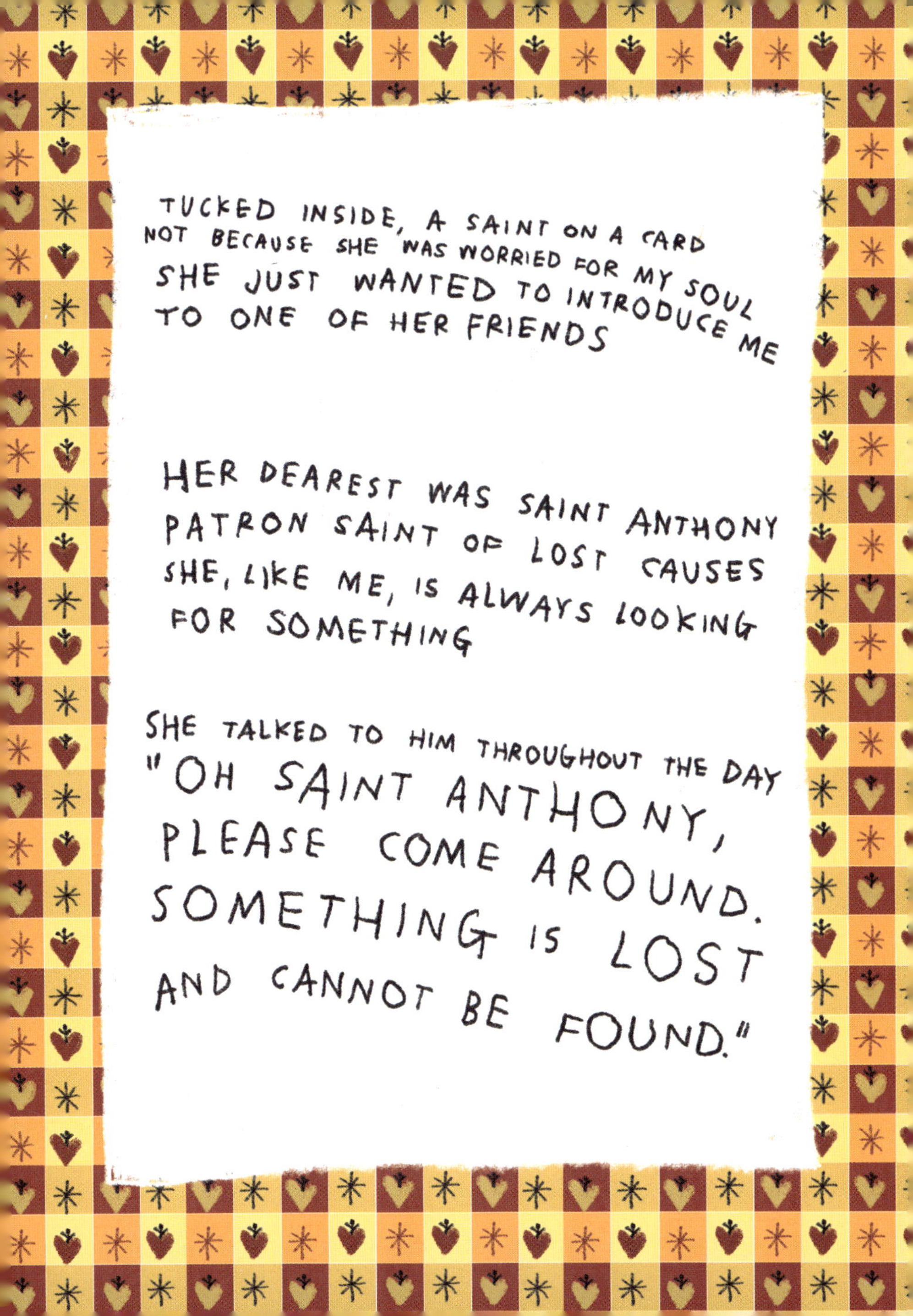
TUCKED INSIDE, A SAINT ON A CARD
NOT BECAUSE SHE WAS WORRIED FOR MY SOUL
SHE JUST WANTED TO INTRODUCE ME
TO ONE OF HER FRIENDS
HER DEAREST WAS SAINT ANTHONY
PATRON SAINT OF LOST CAUSES
SHE, LIKE ME, IS ALWAYS LOOKING
FOR SOMETHING
SHE TALKED TO HIM THROUGHOUT THE DAY
"OH SAINT ANTHONY,
PLEASE COME AROUND.
SOMETHING IS LOST
AND CANNOT BE FOUND."

I LIKE THAT ANTHONY HAS ALWAYS BEEN THERE IN THE ROOM WITH HER, WHEREVER SHE IS, BECAUSE I'VE WONDERED IF SHE WAS LONELY WHEN SHE WAS POSTPARTUM LIKE ME

SHE WENT THROUGH POST-PARTUM 5 TIMES, DURING MID-CENTURY-JUNE-CLEAVER SEXISM, NO LESS

WHEN THE WORLD TOLD HER THAT SHE WASN'T ENOUGH (MOTHERS ARE ALWAYS SOMEHOW NEVER ENOUGH),

DID SHE FALL TO PIECES?

DID SHE STAGE A COUP?

DID SHE TRY TO FIT IN WITH LIPSTICK AND PANTYHOSE? OR DID SHE SMOKE A CIGARETTE ON THE PORCH WITH ANTHONY IN HER ROBE & SLIPPERS?

SINCE I CAN'T ASK HER THESE QUESTIONS, AND SHE CAN'T MAIL ME AN ENVELOPE WITH HER PERFECTLY SINCERE, UNPOLISHED, AND ELEGANT POETRY INSIDE,

I'D LIKE TO OFFER YOU THIS:

I'VE STORED UP SOME OF THE LOVE SHE GAVE ME

I HAVE PLENTY TO SHARE

IF SHE WAS ABLE, HERE'S WHAT I THINK SHE'D SAY TO ME (US)

Lovey,

I hope this finds you in bed and that you and baby are well fed
that your body is healing and you weren't up all night
here is a saint to talk to when things need to be said
when your thoughts are dark and you don't know how to make them light

they'll go in for the kill, compare you to moms who aren't real
so they can't judge if you're caught talking to saints up above
so talk to this saint - tell her * exactly * how you feel
let it all out so there's room to think to yourself,
"wow. isn't it so nice to be loved?"

Yours always,
Baba ♡

PS: falling to pieces, staging a coup, buying a new lipstick, and smoking a cigarette in your robe are all perfectly appropriate responses when the world tells you that you aren't enough. (you are.)

PATRON SAINT OF
IT'S OK THAT YOUR
LIFE IS A MESS

IT'S SLOW,
BUT I AM

FINDING MY WAY BACK TO MYSELF ♥

GHOSTS IN THE BREASTMILK

BETWEEN MY LOVE FOR HOMEMADE FOOD AND ALSO NUDITY, I THOUGHT—NO, I *KNEW*—THAT I WOULD BREASTFEED. BETWEEN MY INCLINATION TOWARD IT & THAT OLD ADAGE "BREAST IS BEST," IT WAS OBVIOUS TO ME.

SO I BREASTFED.

ALL OF THE MECHANICS WERE WORKING FINE, BESIDES A TRICKY FIRST WEEK OF LEARNING HOW TO LATCH (READ: PLACE ENTIRE BOOB IN MOUTH), A COUPLE OF CLOGGED DUCTS, AND CHAPPED NIPPIES.

MY BABY WAS EATING AND MY BOOBS (MOSTLY THE LEFT ONE) WERE MAKING MILK.

BUT... IT ALL FELT HAUNTED FROM THE VERY BEGINNING. I DIDN'T KNOW HOW TO SAY THIS OR IF THIS WAS AN OK THING TO SAY AT ALL.

I PLAYED IT OUT IN MY HEAD: "AH, YES, HELLO, LACTATION PROFESSIONAL! DURING FEEDINGS, I AM EXPERIENCING A VAGUE BUT OVERWHELMING SENSE OF BEING CHASED BY GHOSTS THAT I DID NOT INVITE INTO MY HOUSE. DO YOU HAVE A PAMPHLET OR MAYBE AN OINTMENT FOR THAT?

THIS SOUNDED LESS LIKE A POSTPARTUM ISSUE AND MORE LIKE A TWILIGHT ZONE EPISODE, SO I JUST KEPT QUIET WHILE MY LEFT BOOB KEPT MY BABY FED.

THE HAUNTED FEELING CONTINUED AND CAUSED CONFUSION WITH MY PARTNER. "I THINK SHE'S HUNGRY," HE'D SAY GENTLY WHILE SHE FUSSED. AND BEFORE EVEN THINKING I WOULD SNAP BACK, "NO, SHE ISN'T."

I MEAN...
SHE WAS A TINY INFANT IN THE THROES OF VERY TYPICAL CLUSTER FEEDING. OF COURSE SHE WAS FUCKING HUNGRY. IF I TOLD HIM THAT IT WAS ONE OF THE GHOSTS WHO SNAPPED AT HIM AND NOT ME, WOULD HE HAVE THOUGHT I WAS IN A HALLUCINATORY HAZE? OR, MAYBE WORSE, IF I *DIDN'T* TELL HIM, WOULD HE HAVE THOUGHT I HAD TERRIBLE MATERNAL INSTINCTS IN REGARD TO KEEPING A BABY ALIVE WITH FOOD?

AS TIME WENT ON, THE GHOSTS' VISITS BECAME PREDICTABLE: WHEN MY MILK LET DOWN, THEY WOULD SHOW UP. A DARK NUMBNESS WOULD TAKE HOLD. IT FELT SO VERY... WRONG. HOW COULD SOMETHING SO NATURAL AND SO LOVELY MAKE ME FEEL SO TERRIBLE?

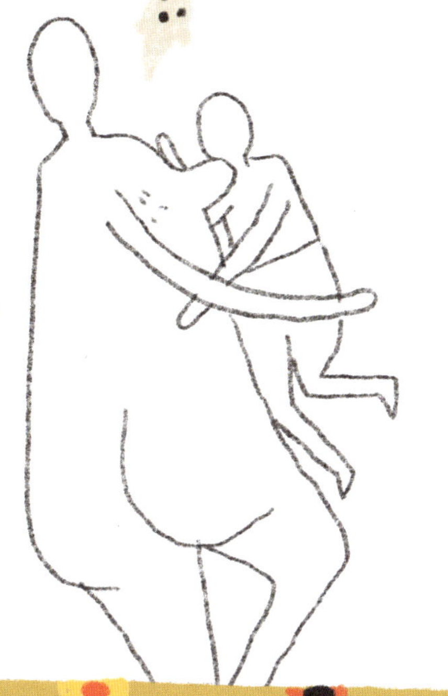

I HAD NEVER HEARD ANYONE DESCRIBE BREASTFEEDING THIS WAY. I HAD HEARD DIFFERENT *PARTS* OF BREASTFEEDING HAD THE POTENTIAL TO FEEL TERRIBLE. LIKE THE PHYSICAL TOLL, ENORMOUS TIME COMMITMENT, SUPPLY ISSUES, ETC. BUT I HAD NEVER HEARD SOMEONE JUST COME OUT AND SAY: "NOPE. HATED IT. MADE ME FEEL AWFUL." NOT EVEN A FLIRTY "NOT FOR ME" FOLLOWED BY A KIND WINK.

THE PEOPLE WHO DIDN'T LOVE IT, WELL, MAYBE THEY EXISTED, BUT THEY DIDN'T VOLUNTEER THIS INFO. I WONDER IF THAT'S BECAUSE THEY, LIKE ME, FELT ODDLY ASHAMED. BUT WHY DO THEY FEEL ASHAMED?

I FELT ASHAMED BECAUSE I THOUGHT THE GHOSTS WERE PROOF THAT I WAS CRAZY AND/OR BAD.

BUT YOU KNOW WHAT'S ACTUALLY CRAZY AND BAD?

THE EXPECTATIONS AND CULTURE AROUND MOTHERHOOD THAT MADE ME FEEL THAT WAY IN THE FIRST PLACE. THAT ABSOLUTE CLUSTER-FUCK OF COMPETING INFORMATION ABOUT POST-PARTUM DELIVERED AS MORAL ABSOLUTES.

IT'S CLEAR TO ME NOW: I GET THAT HAUNTED, DARK, NUMB FEELING WHEN MY EXPERIENCE ISN'T WHAT I EXPECTED IT TO BE. I SEE GHOSTS WHEN I FEEL LIKE I'M FUCKING IT UP SOMEHOW AND I *SHOULD* BE FEELING AND ACTING DIFFERENTLY. MAYBE THE GHOSTS ARE FRIENDS THAT ARE HERE TO HELP ME IDENTIFY THE WAYS THAT I DON'T FIT.

IT FEELS SPOOKY BECAUSE IT'S UNEXPECTED. IT FELT SPOOKY TO HATE BREASTFEEDING BECAUSE I TRULY THOUGHT THAT I WOULD LOVE IT.

BUT I DIDN'T.

SO I STOPPED.

I WENT ON TO BREASTFEED A TINY BIT HERE AND THERE TO STAY COMFORTABLE, MAYBE IN THE MORNING OR AT NIGHT. AND EVERY TIME I WOULD WONDER IF IT WAS OUR *LAST*.

ONE TIME I CRIED BECAUSE I FELT AS BEAUTIFUL AS A KLIMT PAINTING BECAUSE WE HAD JUST BATHED, AND IN EARLY POSTPARTUM, BATHED = FULL GLAM. I AM GLAD I HAVE THIS PICTURE IN MY HEAD.

EVENTUALLY THE LAST TIME HAPPENED BUT I DON'T REMEMBER IT.

THE GHOSTS DIDN'T VISIT WHEN I WOULD CURL UP INTO A CUTE LITTLE PILE ON THE COUCH WITH CRICKET AND HER BOTTLE. INSTEAD, MAYBE MY PIT BULL OR CAT WOULD VISIT OR I'D CALL MY SISTER OR DO A CROSSWORD.

THE DARK HAUNTED FEELING WAS REPLACED BY A LIGHT-HEARTED MUNDANITY.

EVEN THOUGH IT'S NOT FOR ME, *INSERT KIND WINK HERE* I STILL LOVE HOMEMADE FOOD & NUDITY SO MUCH. IF I SEE YOU OUT IN THE WORLD BREASTFEEDING, YOU'LL KNOW IT'S ME 'CAUSE I WILL SMILE AT YOU LIKE I AM A KID AND YOU ARE A SPARKLY MAGICIAN WHO JUST PULLED A RABBIT OUT OF YOUR HAT.

SO I FIXED THAT OLD POSTER THAT I'VE SEEN IN THE OB-GYN OFFICE:

BREASTS ~~IS BEST.~~
ARE COOL.
IF YOU HAVE THEM, AND ARE ABLE TO, YOU MAY WANT TO USE THEM TO FEED YOUR CHILD. IF YOU DON'T HAVE THEM, DON'T WANT TO USE THEM TO FEED YOUR CHILD, OR ARE UNABLE TO DO SO, YOU ALSO DESERVE A POSTER.♥

"FERTILITY"
"SO... WILL YOU
HAVE ANOTHER?"
A PROPHECY DISGUISED
AS A QUESTION
DROPS ME INTO AN
ANCIENT SCRIPT I DIDN'T
AUDITION FOR

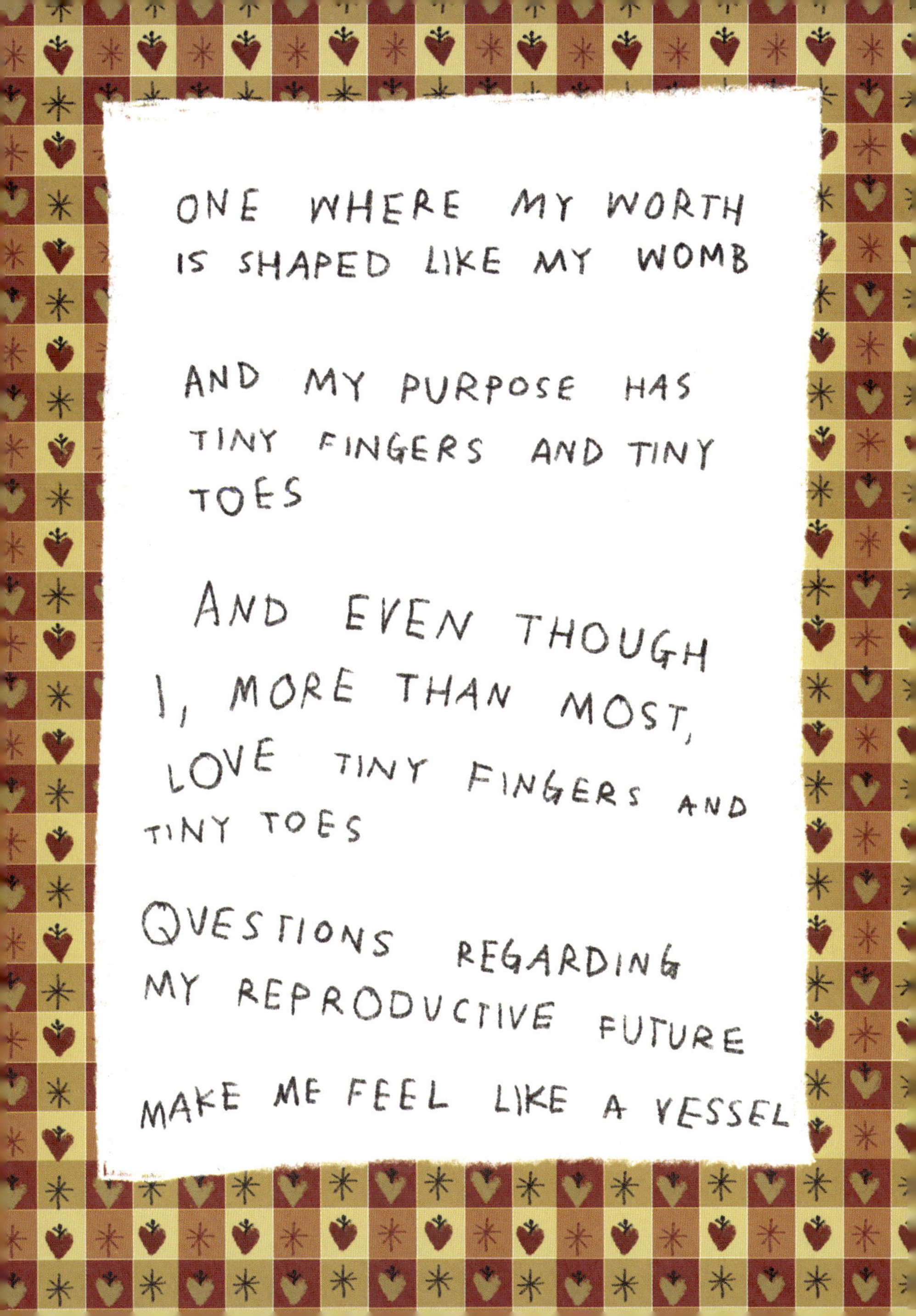
ONE WHERE MY WORTH
IS SHAPED LIKE MY WOMB
AND MY PURPOSE HAS
TINY FINGERS AND TINY
TOES
AND EVEN THOUGH
I, MORE THAN MOST,
LOVE TINY FINGERS AND
TINY TOES
QUESTIONS REGARDING
MY REPRODUCTIVE FUTURE
MAKE ME FEEL LIKE A VESSEL

OR A PLOT DEVICE

IN THE STORY THAT I DIDN'T WRITE

I WAS ASKED ABOUT MY REPRODUCTIVE ASPIRATIONS LONG BEFORE I HAD SORTED OUT MY PERSONAL & PROFESSIONAL ASPIRATIONS

AND THE QUESTIONS KEPT COMING AS I BUILT OUT MY LIFE AND MY CAREER.

I KNOW THAT THE QUESTIONS ARE AND HAVE BEEN BORNE OUT OF LOVE

BUT THEY WERE ROOTED IN AN OBLIGATION TO A LIFE PATH THAT I HAD NEVER PUBLICLY OR PRIVATELY COMMITTED TO

WHICH IS WHY THE QUESTIONS WERE JARRING

THEY LEFT ME WONDERING,

DID THEY THINK I WAS BORED? DID THEY THINK I WAS LONELY? THAT I LACKED PURPOSE?

IT DIDN'T TAKE MUCH TO SEE THAT MY LIFE WAS FULL

THAT I LOVED AND WAS LOVED

AND THAT I WAS HOPELESSLY DETERMINED TO BE AN ARTIST

OR

MAYBE THE QUESTIONS
HAD NOTHING TO DO
WITH ME AT ALL

MAYBE THEY HAD
MORE TO DO WITH THE
PERSON ASKING THEM

A LACK OF IMAGINATION
OR AN EARNEST MISTAKE
ASSUMING WHAT MADE
YOU HAPPY WILL MAKE SOMEONE
ELSE HAPPY TOO

DID THEY FORGET THAT THERE ARE A MILLION THINGS WE COULD HOPE FOR?
THAT THERE ARE A MILLION THINGS WE COULD CREATE WITH THE LIFE FORCE WE HAVE INSIDE?

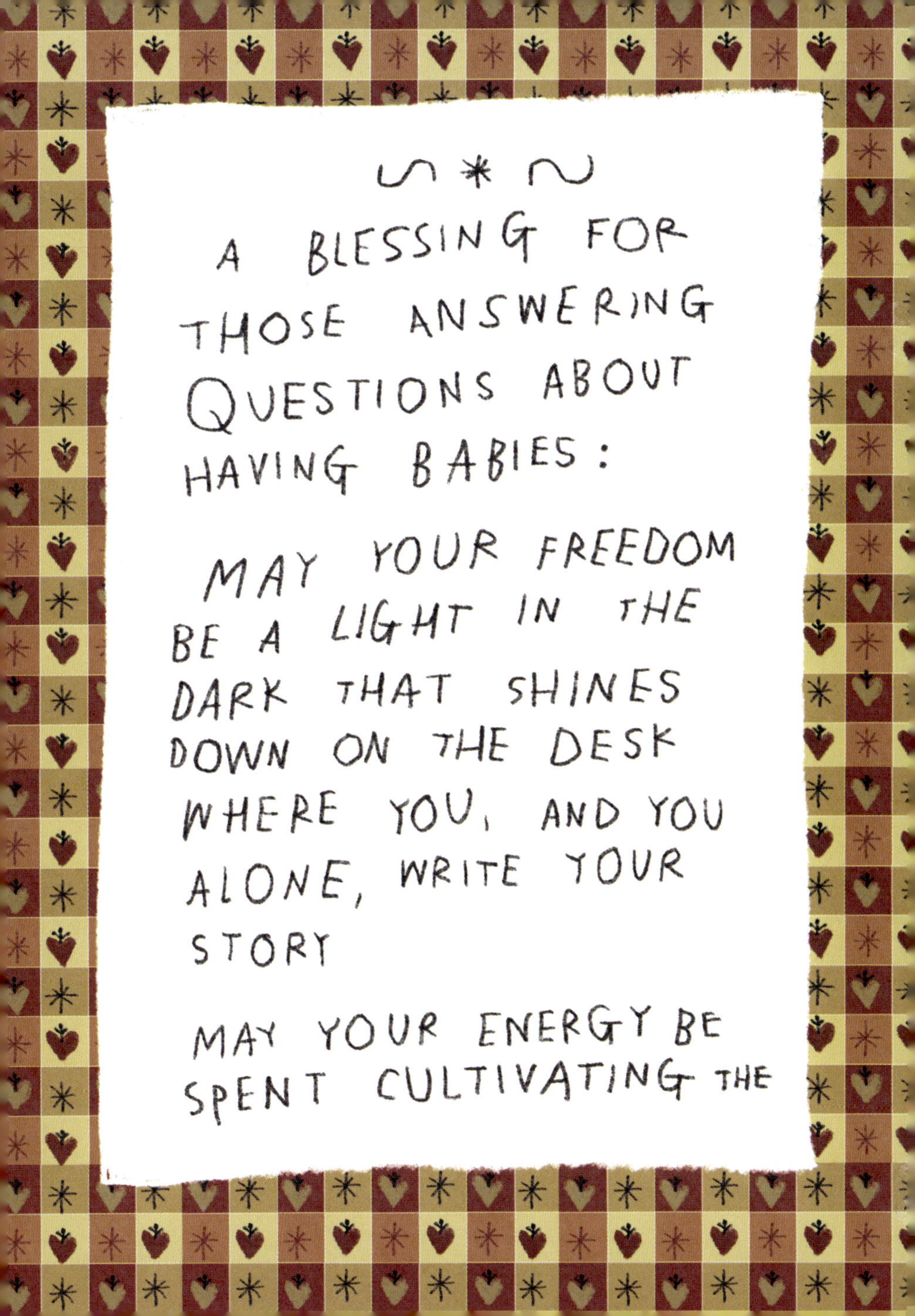
A BLESSING FOR
THOSE ANSWERING
QUESTIONS ABOUT
HAVING BABIES:
MAY YOUR FREEDOM
BE A LIGHT IN THE
DARK THAT SHINES
DOWN ON THE DESK
WHERE YOU, AND YOU
ALONE, WRITE YOUR
STORY
MAY YOUR ENERGY BE
SPENT CULTIVATING THE

LIFE YOU WANT INSTEAD OF SPENT DISMANTLING THE LIFE THAT OTHERS WANT FOR YOU.

MAY YOU BE GIVEN TIME AND SPACE TO FIGURE OUT WHAT YOU WANT IF YOU NEED IT

AND GIVEN RESPECT IF YOU DON'T

MAY YOUR WORTH—
YOUR ENOUGHNESS—

BE ON DISPLAY BUT
UNTOUCHABLE
LIKE AN ANCIENT RELIC
PROTECTED BY GLASS &
VELVET ROPES
MAY YOUR LIFE BE
A TESTAMENT TO THE
LIFE-SAVING ACT OF
CHOOSING WHAT IS
TRUE INSTEAD OF
CHOOSING WHAT WAS
CHOSEN FOR YOU.

A BLESSING FOR THOSE ASKING QUESTIONS ABOUT WHETHER OR NOT SOMEONE WILL HAVE A BABY:

MAY YOUR QUESTIONS CREATE SPACE FOR THE PERSON ANSWERING THEM

MAY ANY THOUGHTS YOU HAVE ON THE SUBJECT BE PUT ON THE SHELF UNTIL YOU ARE ASKED TO SHARE THEM.

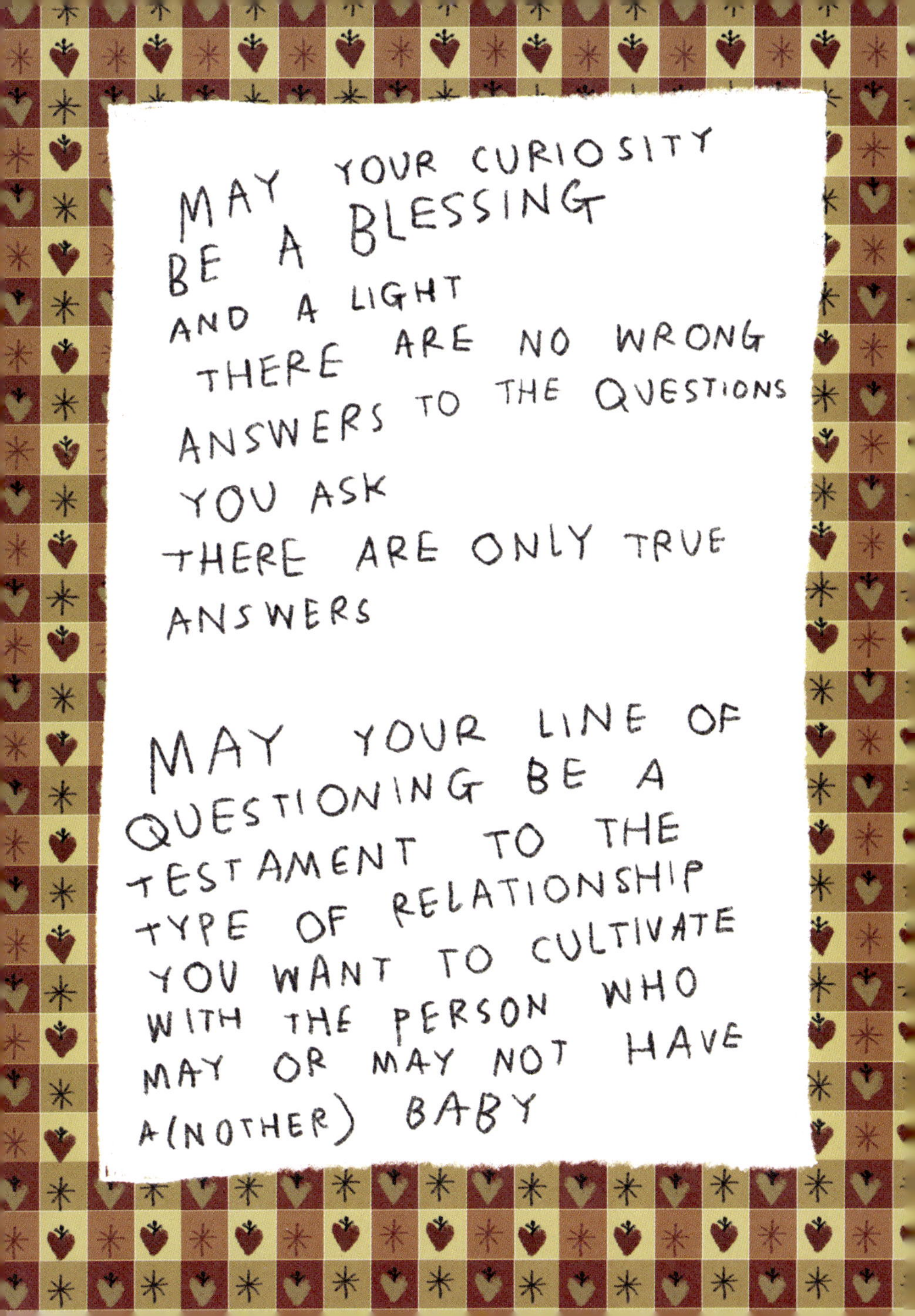
MAY YOUR CURIOSITY
BE A BLESSING
AND A LIGHT
THERE ARE NO WRONG
ANSWERS TO THE QUESTIONS
YOU ASK
THERE ARE ONLY TRUE
ANSWERS
MAY YOUR LINE OF
QUESTIONING BE A
TESTAMENT TO THE
TYPE OF RELATIONSHIP
YOU WANT TO CULTIVATE
WITH THE PERSON WHO
MAY OR MAY NOT HAVE
A(NOTHER) BABY

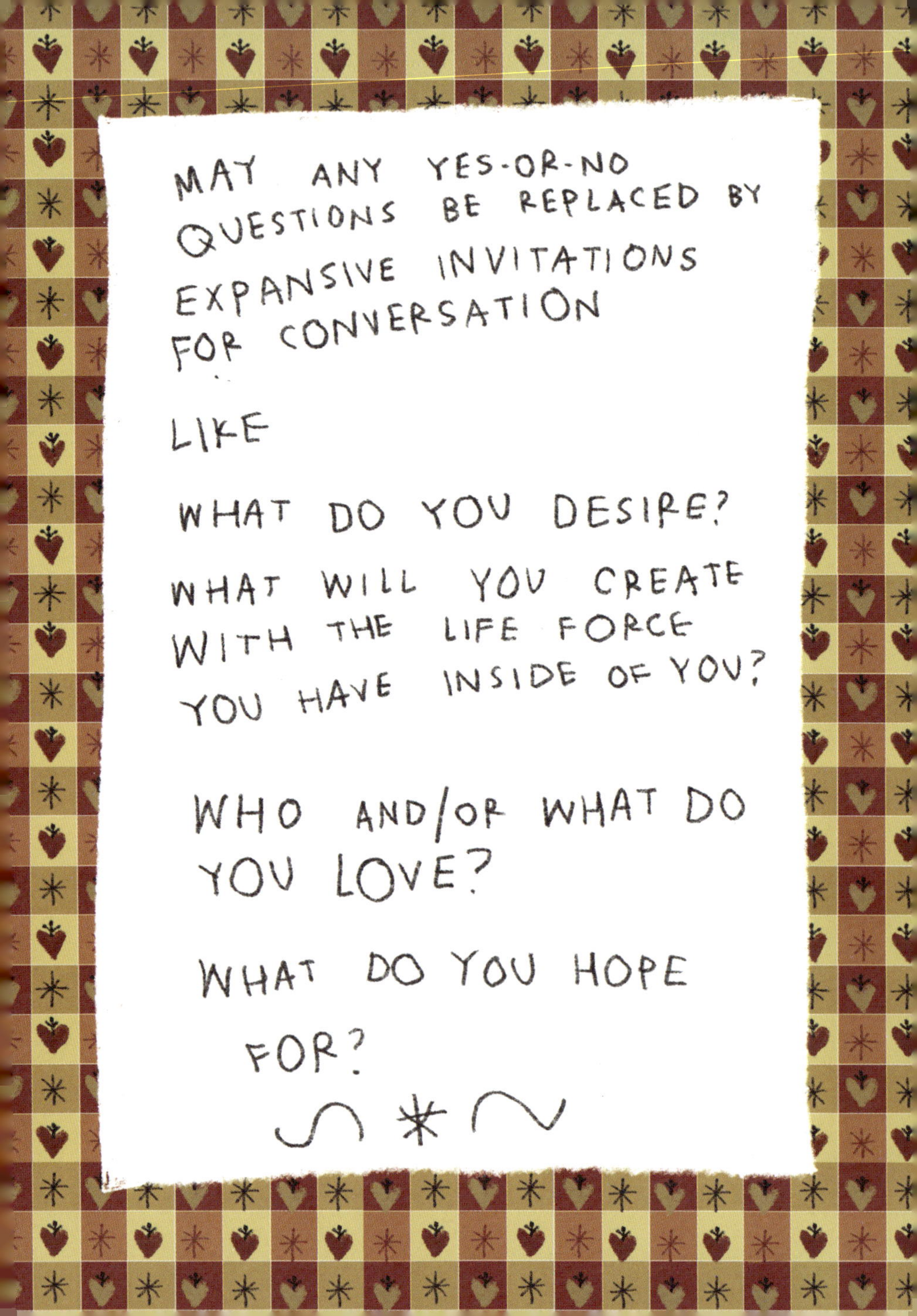
MAY ANY YES-OR-NO
QUESTIONS BE REPLACED BY
EXPANSIVE INVITATIONS
FOR CONVERSATION
LIKE
WHAT DO YOU DESIRE?
WHAT WILL YOU CREATE
WITH THE LIFE FORCE
YOU HAVE INSIDE OF YOU?
WHO AND/OR WHAT DO
YOU LOVE?
WHAT DO YOU HOPE
FOR?

DID YOU KNOW THAT IF YOU PUT THE WORD "FERTILITY" INTO DIRECT SUNLIGHT IT BECOMES A PRISM

THE LIGHT DISPERSES INTO A MILLION LITTLE RAINBOWS

REVEALING ITS COMPLEXITY

THERE ARE A MILLION POSSIBILITIES

A MILLION WAYS TO BRING SOMETHING GOOD INTO THE WORLD

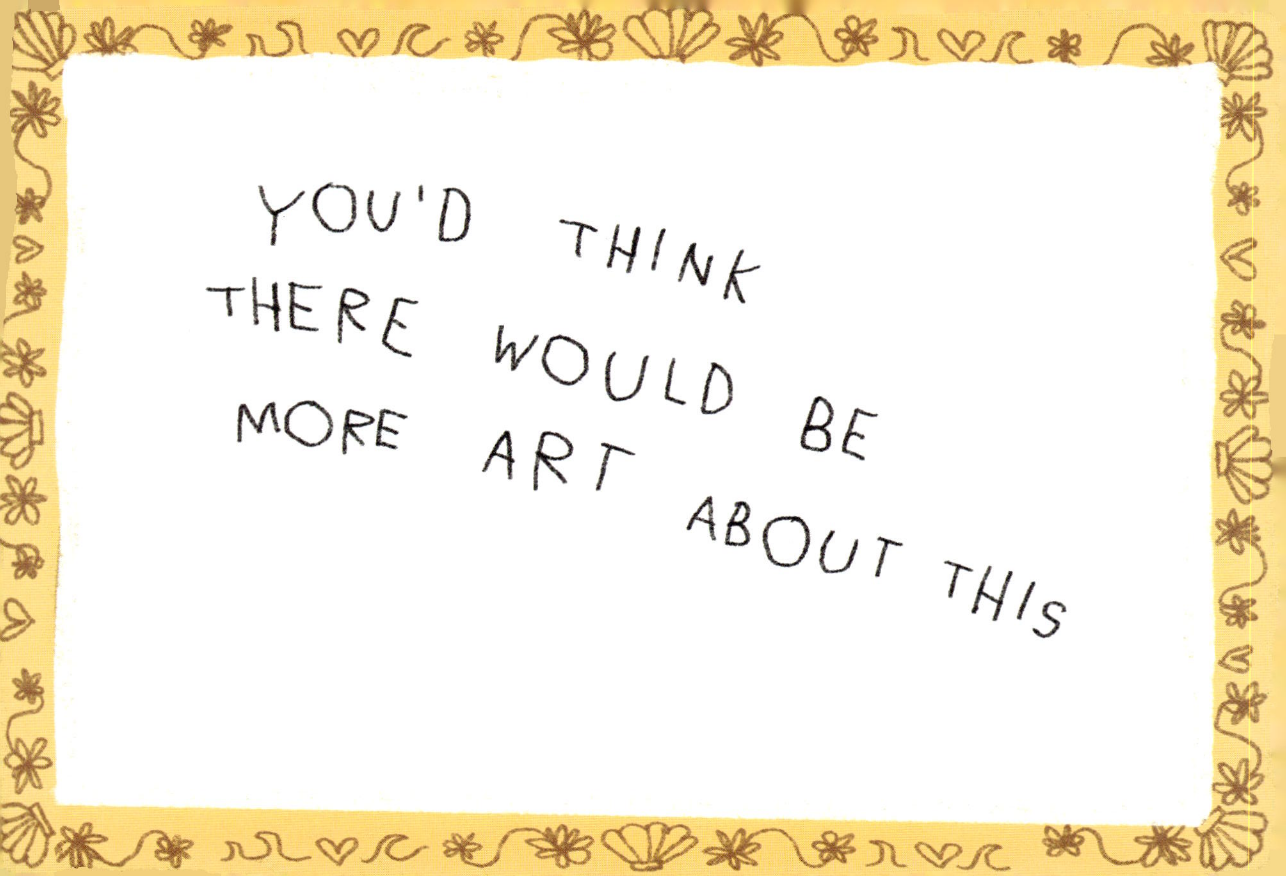
YOU'D THINK
THERE WOULD BE
MORE ART ABOUT THIS

PART 3: TL;DR

HOW DO I RECONCILE THE DICHOTOMY BETWEEN HOW THIS LOOKS AND HOW THIS FEELS?

CALL ME SHEWOLF,
SOFT AND WILD,
BOTH TRUE, SO THAT I
CAN REMEMBER SIMPLE
CARE TASKS AREN'T SIMPLE.
THEY'RE THE FIRST STEP TO
OVERTHROW THE KING.

IF THERE ARE GHOSTS, THEY'RE TRYING TO TELL YOU SOMETHING THAT'S TRUE.

THERE ARE A MILLION THINGS WE COULD HOPE FOR.

THERE ARE A MILLION THINGS WE COULD CREATE WITH THE LIFE FORCE WE HAVE INSIDE.

WHAT DO YOU DESIRE?
WHAT WILL YOU CREATE?

PART 4:

THE WILD SEA & ME

WILL MY NEW LIFE
SWALLOW ME WHOLE?
THE OCEAN,
~ MY NEW LIFE ~,
IS TERRIFYING AND
AWE-INSPIRING AT
THE SAME TIME. SO
MUCH CHAOS AND SO
MUCH BEAUTY BENEATH
THE SURFACE.

THE WILD SEA IS IN A
CONSTANT STATE OF
TRANSFORMATION ~ EACH
WAVE THAT CRASHES
RESHAPES THE SHORE.

WILL I GET LOST IN THE EXPANSE?

WILL I EVER FEEL LIKE MYSELF AGAIN IF MY NEW LIFE REQUIRES ME TO BE IN A CONSTANT STATE OF TRANSFORMATION?

CAN I LEARN TO FLOAT WHEN MY INSTINCT IS TO FIGHT?

A SELKIE STORY:

AN OLD FOLKTALE AS REMEMBERED AND ALSO EMBELLISHED BY RANI

I SAW HER—
THE SELKIE IN THE WILD SEA.
SHE WAS A SILVER SEAL
EQUAL PARTS POWERFUL & SOFT
DANCING IN THE DARK WAVES

ON LAND SHE COULD SHED HER
SEAL SKIN

AND BECOME A HUMAN WOMAN

A WALKING DISPLAY OF
MYTHICAL ALCHEMY

NAKED AND CURIOUS, TOES
IN THE SAND.

ONE DAY SHE SWAM ASHORE

LEFT HER SEAL SKIN ON THE
BEACH

TO STAND IN THE SEAGRASS
WHILE IT DANCED IN THE WIND

TICKLING HER FINGERTIPS

A FISHERMAN WALKS BY
HER BEAUTY KNOCKS THE AIR FROM HIS LUNGS
IN A GASPING PANIC
HE STEALS HER SKIN AND LOCKS IT AWAY
FORCING HER TO LIVE ON LAND
AS A HUMAN FOREVER

THEY GET MARRIED
THE LANDLOCKED SELKIE AND THE FISHERMAN
SHE HAS HIS CHILDREN
BUILDS A BEAUTIFUL AND LOVING HOME
BUT NEVER FEELS BEAUTIFUL
OR AT HOME IN IT

HER CHILDREN WATCH HER
WHILE SHE STANDS IN THE WINDOW
WATCHING THE SEA
HER EYES ON THE HORIZON
SHE WONDERS
WILL I EVER BE FULLY ALIVE?

ONE DAY SHE OPENS A DUSTY CHEST
IN THE ATTIC
AND FINDS HER SILVER SKIN INSIDE
SO POWERFUL AND SO SOFT
SHE CARRIES IT TO THE OCEAN
THE WAY SHE'D CARRIED
HER CHILDREN THERE
A THOUSAND TIMES BEFORE

SHE STEPS INTO HER SILVER SKIN
WEEPS FOR HER CHILDREN
CALLS OUT THEIR NAMES
AND DISAPPEARS INTO THE DARK WAVES.
THE PULL OF THE WILD SEA
IS IMPOSSIBLE TO RESIST
AND HER CHILDREN CAN HEAR HER
SINGING FROM THE SEA
IN THE NIGHT

HER CHILDREN GROW UP
& INHERIT HER RESTLESS LONGING
THEY WATCH THE HORIZON
FROM THEIR WINDOW AND WONDER
WILL I EVER FEEL FULLY ALIVE?
WILL I EVER FEEL BEAUTIFUL?
WILL I EVER FEEL AT HOME?

THEY SEARCH FOR ANSWERS
LOOKING FOR WHO THEY ARE
& WHY THEY CAN'T SHAKE
THAT FEELING AT THE WINDOW
ONE DAY THEY OPEN A DUSTY CHEST
IN THE ATTIC
AND FIND THEIR OWN SKINS INSIDE
SILVER LIKE THE SEAL
WHO SINGS TO THEM IN THE MOONLIGHT

AND WHEN THAT RESTLESS FEELING RETURNS
THEY KNOW IT'S THE CALL
OF THE WILD SEA
THEY KNOW EXACTLY WHAT TO DO
SHE SHOWED THEM HOW
THEY DIVE IN
AND DANCE IN THE
DARK WAVES
WITH THEIR MOM

I SAW THEM THE OTHER DAY
SILVER SEALS
SPARKLING IN THE SUN
ON A ROCK JUST BEYOND THE SHORE
ONE WAS RESTING THEIR HEAD
ON THEIR MOTHER'S SOFT BELLY
WHILE THE OTHER
LOOKED OUT AT THE HORIZON

FROM THERE ON THE BEACH
I FELT MY OWN FAMILIAR
RESTLESS LONGING
CRYSTAL CLEAR AGAINST
THE BACKDROP
OF THE ABSENCE OF THEIRS
I WONDERED
WILL I EVER BE FULLY ALIVE?
WILL I EVER FEEL BEAUTIFUL?
WILL I EVER FEEL AT HOME?

I ALWAYS THOUGHT
THE LONGING AND THE QUESTIONS
WERE A CURSE
AND THEY'VE BECOME
MASSIVELY INCONVENIENT
SINCE MY DAUGHTER WAS BORN

MAYBE IT'S TRUE THAT I'M BROKEN,
A TRAGIC LANDLOCKED HUMAN
WITH SAND IN HER TOES
FINGERTIPS IN THE SEAGRASS
LOOKING FOR
MYTHICAL THINGS

BUT DEEP DOWN I KNOW
MY RESTLESS LONGING
IS THE WILD SEA
TELLING ME
THAT I AM WORTHY
OF FEELING FULLY ALIVE
OF FEELING BEAUTIFUL
(BECAUSE BEAUTY = TRUTH)
OF FEELING AT HOME
(A PLACE WHERE MY FULL SELF IS SAFE)

AND IF THAT IS TRUE
(& THE WILD SEA NEVER LIES)
I MUST NEVER STOP SEARCHING
FOR MY WILDEST, TRUEST SELF
AND FOLLOW HER
WHERE SHE TAKES ME
BECAUSE THE STAKES
ARE TOO HIGH

IF I DON'T
HOW WILL MY DAUGHTER
KNOW WHAT TO DO
WHEN SHE HEARS HER OWN
CALL OF THE WILD SEA?
HOW WILL SHE KNOW
THAT THE RESTLESS LONGING
IS HER TRUEST SELF
ASKING HER TO DO
WHAT IT TAKES
TO BE FREE?

KITCHEN SINK BATHS

THE FIRST THING I LEARNED ABOUT HER WAS THAT SHE LOVED WATER

I BATHED HER IN THE KITCHEN SINK WITH LAVENDER SOAP AND A LITTLE TINY WASHCLOTH

THAT I MADE FOR HER
WITH COTTON YARN

I WONDERED WHO'D
SHE BE WHEN I
MADE IT

WHAT WILL SHE LOVE?

THEN, WHILE USING IT
TO WASH HER TINY
HEAD AND TINY BODY,
I LEARNED THAT
FIRST THING

WE FELL IN LOVE
ON AN UNMADE BED
WITH YELLOW LINEN SHEETS

THE BED SAT BY THE
WINDOW, AND SHE
AND MY CAT WOULD
NAP AND STRETCH IN
THE SUN.
"OOOOOOH
BIG STRETCH,"
I'D SAY TO THEM BOTH

FOR A TIME THEY WERE BOTH THE EXACT SAME SIZE ~ A FLEETING DETAIL THAT MADE ME FEEL ACHY ALL OVER

WILL I GET BETTER AT THIS? WITNESSING HER GROWTH AND HAVING TO LET A VERSION OF HER GO?

FOR THOSE MONTHS,
MY BODY DIDN'T FEEL
LIKE MY BODY AT ALL,
MORE LIKE AN OLD
AIR MATTRESS WITH
A SLOW LEAK

MY BOOBS LOOKED
LIKE BLUEBERRY
MUFFINS FRESH FROM
THE OVEN:

ONE PUFFED UP AND GORGEOUS & THE OTHER DEFLATED

EVERY ATOM OF MY BEING FELT LIKE I WAS BEING REARRANGED

AROUND HER

HOW DO I TEND TO
AND LOVE MYSELF
WHEN I DON'T KNOW
WHO THAT SELF IS?

I'M SLIPPING

THROUGH MY

FINGERS

WE SPENT POSTPARTUM IN A BIG OLD FARMHOUSE THAT MY BOYFRIEND AND I BOUGHT A FEW YEARS BEFORE CRICKET CAME

IT HAD BURIED CHARM UNDER LAYERS OF BAD CHOICES MADE IN THE '90s

A FIXER-UPPER THAT REQUIRED IMAGINATION AND GRIT TO SEE THAT IT COULD BE FIXED UP AT ALL

I LIKE THAT IT WAS
HER FIRST HOME

IT WAS IN NEED OF
SOME SERIOUS LOVE,
WHICH WE GAVE TO
IT WHILE WE PEELED
BACK ITS LAYERS

THERE WERE NO WALLS
IN THE ENTRYWAY THE
DAY WE BROUGHT HER
HOME, WHICH FELT
LIKE POETRY

MAYBE OUR NEW LIFE
TOGETHER IS LIKE
THE WATER SHE LOVES

CONSTANT RENEWAL

TIME SLIPPING THROUGH
MY FINGERS
I THINK

I'LL ALWAYS FEEL ACHY
ALL OVER WHEN THE
TIDE GOES OUT, THEN
COMES BACK IN.
AND IT TAKES A LOT
OF IMAGINATION AND
GRIT TO FIND PEACE
IN MOTION

THE KITCHEN SINK
BATHS, CAT STRETCHES,
MUFFIN BOOBS, AND
OUR OLD HOUSE
REMIND ME THAT
LOVE IS IN THE
FLEETING DETAILS.
I WANT TO NOTICE
AS MANY OF THEM
AS POSSIBLE

AS THE WATER GOES
OUT, AND COMES BACK
IN,

MOURNING WHAT
WAS AND HOPING
FOR WHAT WILL
BE

AT THE
SAME
TIME

ORANGE FISH

I GET THE CRAYONS AND PRINTER PAPER OUT & PUT THEM ON THE DIRTY RUG ON THE DIRTY FLOOR.

WE SIT DOWN TO DRAW PICTURES TOGETHER.

AND BY THAT I MEAN, I SIT ON THE FLOOR AND IMMEDIATELY FALL INTO A VORTEX OF CRAYONS.

IT'S BLISS!

BIG, BAD DRAWINGS ON WRINKLED PAPER! OH THE FREEDOM & JOY OF DRAWING FROM A PURE PLACE. NO EXPECTATIONS. THIS IS JUST PURELY A TERRIBLE DRAWING OF AN ORANGE FISH THAT I ENTITLED "ORANGE FISH"

I AM LIVING OUT A DREAM THAT I HAVE HAD TUCKED AWAY IN MY HEART.

TO SIT ON THE FLOOR AND DRAW WITH MY KID

~ SUSPENDED IN TIME, AS IF FLOATING IN WATER ~

JUST FOR A MINUTE.

AS I MOVE ON TO DRAWING A SEAHORSE, AN OCTOPUS,  AND A WHALE,

I REALIZE THAT MY KID HAD GOTTEN UP AND WALKED AWAY.

I MEAN, SHE'S 12 MONTHS OLD AND DOES NOT GIVE A SINGLE SHIT ABOUT DRAWING.

SHE'S POURING CHEERIOS INTO THE BACK OF HER DUMP TRUCK AND THEN INTO A HOUSEPLANT.

SHE DID NOT DRAW ON THE PAPER I GAVE HER. IT SITS BLANK NEXT TO MY OWN PERSONAL RUG GALLERY. "I SHOULD SIGN THOSE," I THINK TO MYSELF.

SHE SMILES AT ME PROUDLY AS SHE'S PUTTING A HANDFUL OF POTTING SOIL CHEERIOS INTO HER SHOES. SHE ONLY HAS 4 TEETH AND ALL OF THEM ARE ORANGE BECAUSE SHE TOOK A PRETTY SOLID BITE OUT OF HER CRAYON AT SOME POINT WHILE I WAS DRAWING.

& RIGHT AS SHE SCOOPS SOME OF THE POTTING SOIL CHEERIOS OUT OF HER SHOE AND INTO HER MOUTH

I REALIZE:

THIS DREAM I HAD TUCKED AWAY WAS WRONG.

IT'S NOT TO SIT ON THE FLOOR AND DRAW WITH MY KID.

MY DREAM IS WHATEVER THE FUCK THIS IS

MY DREAM IS TO LOVE
MY KID SO MUCH THAT
WHEN WE DO THINGS
TOGETHER
~TIME IS SUSPENDED,
AS IF FLOATING IN WATER~
JUST FOR A MINUTE.

MY DREAM IS TO FALL
INTO HER VORTEX.

THE DUMP TRUCK CHEERIOS
ARE SUDDENLY SO GORGEOUS
TO ME. A GLIMPSE INTO
WHO THIS PERSON IS
UNDER ALL OF THE LIKES
AND DISLIKES I'VE ALREADY
STARTED TO PROJECT
ONTO HER.

"EVERY NEW THING I LEARN ABOUT YOU MAKES ME LOVE YOU MORE," I SAY.

ONE DAY, THE DUMP TRUCK POTTING SOIL CHEERIOS WILL TURN INTO BIGGER LIKES, DISLIKES, CURIOSITIES, AND INSTINCTS THAT WILL TURN INTO A FULL LIFE THAT SHE WILL CREATE FOR HERSELF.

I WANT TO ACKNOWLEDGE AND CELEBRATE THE WAYS THAT WE'RE DIFFERENT NOW (I LOVE CRAYONS AND YOU LOVE DUMP TRUCKS!! ISN'T THAT WONDERFUL?!) SO THAT SHE KNOWS THAT MY LOVE FOR HER DOES NOT DEPEND ON OUR ALIKENESS.

MY LOVE FOR HER IS PURE. NO EXPECTATIONS.

SHE'S NOT HERE TO FULFILL MY DREAMS.

SHE'S HERE TO FIND HER OWN.

& WHILE SHE DOES,

I'LL BE RIGHT HERE,

SITTING ON MY DIRTY

RUG WITH MY CRAYONS

SAYING,

"EVERY NEW THING I LEARN ABOUT YOU MAKES ME LOVE YOU EVEN MORE"

~FOREVER

PART 4: TL;DR

WILL MY NEW LIFE
SWALLOW ME WHOLE?
I HAVE A RESTLESS FEELING—
LIKE A SELKIE LONGING FOR
THE SEA. THAT FEELING IS MY
TRUEST AND WILDEST SELF
ASKING ME TO DO WHAT IT
TAKES TO BE FREE. I WANT
TO SET MYSELF FREE SO THAT
MY DAUGHTER KNOWS HOW.

THE FIRST THING I LEARNED ABOUT HER WAS THAT SHE LOVED THE WATER. IT MAKES ME ACHY ALL OVER TO WATCH HER GROW AND HAVE TO LET A VERSION OF HER GO. BUT EVERY NEW THING THAT I LEARN ABOUT HER MAKES ME LOVE HER MORE. I WANT TO LEARN NEW THINGS FOREVER. THE TIDE GOES OUT AND THE TIDE COMES BACK IN. CONSTANT RENEWAL, TIME SLIPPING THROUGH MY FINGERS. ♥

OFFBEAT/CREATIVE/REFLECTIVE RECOMMENDATIONS TO FEEL LESS ALONE:
LIFEFORM BY JENNY SLATE
THE BABY ON THE FIRE ESCAPE BY JULIE PHILLIPS
THE ARGONAUTS BY MAGGIE NELSON
THE MOTHERLOAD BY SARAH HOOVER
A LIFE'S WORK BY RACHEL CUSK
ONGOINGNESS BY SARAH MANGUSO
BREASTS AND EGGS BY MIEKO KAWAKAMI
ORDINARY NOTES BY CHRISTINA SHARPE
BLUETS BY MAGGIE NELSON
SPILT MILK BY COURTNEY ZOFFNESS
REVOLUTIONARY MOTHERING EDITED BY ALEXIS PAULINE GUMBS, CHINA MARTENS, AND MAI'A WILLIAMS

HELPFUL/INSIGHTFUL RESOURCES:

EXPECTING BETTER by Emily Oster ♥

CRIBSHEET by Emily Oster

LIKE A MOTHER by Angela Garbes

ESSENTIAL LABOR by Angela Garbes ♥

MATRESCENCE by Lucy Jones ♥

HOW TO KEEP HOUSE WHILE DROWNING by K.C. Davis

NURTURE by Erica Chidi Cohen

THE FOURTH TRIMESTER by Kimberly Ann Johnson

BIRTH WITHOUT FEAR by January Harshe

GUIDEBOOK TO RELATIVE STRANGERS by Camille T. Dungy

GOOD MOMS HAVE SCARY THOUGHTS by Karen Kleiman

RANI BAN IS AN ARTIST AND WRITER BASED IN THE HUDSON VALLEY, WHERE SHE OWNS A (CUTE) ART SUPPLY STORE CALLED THE LITTLE ART SHOP. HER ART IS SOLD IN SHOPS AROUND THE WORLD BUT SHE FEELS MOST ALIVE AT HOME—A 200-YEAR-OLD HOUSE THAT SHE SHARES WITH HER PARTNER, HER KID, AND A FEW RESCUED MISFITS~SOME FURRY, SOME FEATHERED.